# JUST IN TIME!

# STEWARDSHIP SERVICES

## David N. Mosser

Abingdon Press

*Nashville*

JUST IN TIME!
STEWARDSHIP SERVICES

*This book is printed on acid-free paper.*

**Library of Congress Cataloging-in-Publication Data**

Mosser, David, 1952-
    Stewardship services / David N. Mosser.
        p. cm.—(Just in time!)
    Includes bibliographical references and index.
    (pbk. : alk. paper)
ISBN-13: 978-0-687-33516-9
    1. Tithes—Biblical teaching. 2. Christian giving—Biblical teaching. 3. Stewardship, Christian—Biblical teaching. I. Title.

    BS680.T56M67 2006
    248'.6—dc22

                                                                2006013680

07 08 09 10 11 12 13 14 15 16—10 9 8 7 6 5 4 3 2 1
MANUFACTURED IN THE UNITED STATES OF AMERICA

To Ry and Neil

For their unfailing good humor and curiosity about

this splendid world God has given us as a treasured

gift to manage as stewards

With love,

DNM

# CONTENTS

## Contents

# INTRODUCTION

Having been a pastor in local churches for almost thirty years, I know from hard-earned experience that if there is one topic that puts fear into preachers it is standing in the pulpit while addressing the theme of stewardship. Of course, stewardship is, biblically, a much richer word than we have afforded it. Yet, for most rank-and-file church attendees, when preachers say the word "stewardship," the congregation hears the word "money." In this modest volume in the *Just in Time!* series, we have assembled a collection of sermons that tackle the theme of stewardship. To be sure, many of the selected sermons do talk about Christian believers and their relationship to money, but some sermons in this compilation use a more wide-ranging awareness of stewardship.

The English word we use for stewardship comes from the Greek word from which we also derive the word "economy." Essentially stewardship means "to manage the household." It does not mean "own the household." Accurately, and in terms of Christian stewardship, whenever we speak about "owning something" we are using a misnomer. As Christians we believe that God owns everything. Theologically speaking, we merely manage the households God has given us to oversee. Consequently, whatever gifts and graces we *possess*, we do so only in the sense that God owns them and lends them to us to manage.

As mentioned above, the household that comes to mind when we hear the word "stewardship" is the household of money. In reality, however, anything that Christians oversee becomes a household we govern. For example, we are Christian stewards over our influence, faith, time, vote, compassion, spiritual life, listening, prayer, cooking, love, encouragement, good will, and so on. Those who understand stewardship households in this fashion could name hundreds of stewardship households—or more. Indeed anything we manage is a stewardship "household." Clearly our households include our money, but stewardship reaches far beyond the mere concept of money.

I have taken the liberty to select and adapt what I consider the best sermons about stewardship that have appeared over the years in *The Abingdon Preaching Annual.* The sermon writers are as diverse as the sermons, although some Scripture passages are used in more than one sermon. Many of the writers are well known; others labor faithfully in more anonymous vineyards of the Lord. Yet the guiding principle in the selection of these sermons is the question: "Does this sermon help us understand and communicate stewardship to our people in appropriate and understandable ways?"

I have also written worship aids for each of the twenty-four sermons in the collection. To provide for the varied needs of those who use this book, I have included material to cover diverse worship necessities. Included in the worship helps are Calls to Worship, Prayers of Confession and Words of Assurance, Prayers prior to the Offering, Pastoral Prayers, Invocations, Benedictions, and other special-use prayers. It is my hope that preachers will use this new material to "prime the pump" for the preacher's own inspired prayers offered on behalf of the congregation. Words printed in **bold** type in responsive readings are meant to be said in unison, by the whole congregation. Words in regular print are meant to be said by one person—the worship leader or pastor.

A final word about this book and stewardship. In a sense, the principle of Christian giving is the lifeblood of local congregations. There is nothing more "hands-on" in a church's life than deploying a congregation's ministry gifts to the world—or encouraging people to give as disciples. As ministers, few of us have had much formal training in either leading people to volunteer time and talent or in assisting believers to incorporate "giving principles" into their life of faith.

Although few pastors see themselves as "fundraisers," the truth is that, if we neglect this seemingly mundane task, then the body of Christ suffers. In a troubled family, when money issues enter the already troubled picture, then this circumstance turns up the heat of conflict. Churches are no different. As in families, the nearness of believers often creates friction in opinion and practice. When the further strain of money issues enters the fray, the anxiety can elevate in troublesome ways. Whether or not we like it, pastors are the *de facto* leaders in most congregations. As a result, if preachers do not address the need for people to give and offer theological guidance for a healthy relationship with money, then the rest of the congregation will likely overlook it.

The ministry of Christ's church is only as strong as the resources that support it. In this little book, Abingdon offers pastors a resource intended to help lead congregations toward a fuller discernment of Christian stewardship. After all, stewardship is simply discipleship in its working clothes.

David Neil Mosser
2 February 2006

# MAKE YOUR MONEY WORK FOR YOU?

## INVOCATION

Gracious God, as we worship this day, make our worship worthy of your sovereignty over our lives. Help us be honest with each other and you. Help us put away the idols that our world offers us on a daily basis. Help us understand that everything we have, everything we are belongs to you. Let us turn and return to you and worship your holy name in both spirit and in truth. Give us a sense of the majesty of your power and the good judgment to avail ourselves of the mercy you offer us as we pray, sing, and open your Holy Word. Come, Lord Jesus, and make your presence felt among us today. Amen.

## PRAYER BEFORE THE READING OF HOLY SCRIPTURE

O God, who composed our Holy Scripture through the vision, artistry, and lives of great saints, be now present with us as we hear your wonderful words of life. May our Scripture be for us not merely your inspired word; may it be for us your inspiration that breathes into us a path toward life abundant. May we learn that all we have is a trust from you. We pray this in Jesus' name. Amen.

## SCRIPTURE: Luke 16:1-13

## SERMON BRIEF: MAKING YOUR MONEY WORK FOR YOU

This is an unusual text for, on the surface at least, it is a biblical story glorifying a scoundrel. We can hardly pretend the fellow is more. He has been a lazy, do-nothing steward, an accountant who has terribly neglected his master's business, so that it has cost the master a great deal of money. His master finally gets wind of what is going on and decides to fire him. "Turn in your books," he says, "you're finished with me."

The lazy fellow is shocked. He is too old to find another job. Besides, if word gets around that he was fired for being an inadequate steward, he doesn't stand much chance of finding employment anyway. So he gets busy to keep the job he has.

What he does is, by our standards, the most reprehensible part of the story. He goes out among his master's debtors—people who owe him oil and wine and cheese and wheat—and strikes a quick bargain with each of them to pay off the debts at discount rates. Thus the steward makes instant friends of all the debtors so that they praise him to his master, and he pleases the master by suddenly swelling his storehouses with goods. The master knows this fellow is a rascal, but he likes the ingenuity, the *chutzpah*, and reinstates the steward in his job with commendations for his uncommonly good sense.

You know, I never had a Sunday school teacher who dared touch that story. Jesus must have had fun telling it, for it doubtless shocked some people in his day. But what Jesus wanted to get across was the importance of using money in clever ways that would greatly benefit them. "Make friends for yourselves by means of dishonest wealth so that when it is gone, they may welcome you into the eternal homes" (v. 9).

"When it is gone..." That tells you what Jesus thought of money, doesn't it? I know people who have everything they want financially and are very unhappy. They cheat on their spouses, drink too much, work too hard; they are throwing their lives away because their money cannot make them happy.

It wasn't really *his* money, you're thinking. It was the master's money he was using, not his own. Jesus wanted to make the point that it is never our own money we are dealing with; it is always God's money. That's why the fellow in the story is a steward, a person who looks after someone else's property. We are all stewards; we are only caretakers, no matter how much or how little we have.

Some people forget about this, like that rich man Jesus talks about a little later in the same chapter of Luke. He thinks everything he has is really his, so he doesn't bother to share it with the poor man who lies at the gate begging alms. Then he wakes up in hell for misusing what was God's. His mistake, you see, was in not making his money work for him. A lot of it was lying around without doing any good, when it could have been taking care of the poor beggar at the gate.

The Gospel draws a vivid contrast between this foolish man and one wise woman, who appears in chapter 21. Jesus is at the temple and sees a poor woman, clutching two tiny copper coins, come and drop both of them into the treasury. "Truly I tell you," Jesus says, "this poor widow has put in more than anybody, for it was all she had" (see 21:1-4).

Talk about making your money work for you! Only two copper coins and they earned her a place in history. Here she was with her pittance, and she made it work for her as if it were many millions of dollars!

It isn't how much you have in life; it's what you do with it that counts. Everything we have is a trust from God. And the important thing is to learn to use it wisely by sharing it and taking care of God's world. When we do this, we are making an investment in our own souls. (*John Killinger*)

# BENEDICTION

The God of mercy, peace, and hope abide in our hearts and lives from this day forward. May God's spirit move us to be God's people in the world and be people of charity, peace, and hope—today, tomorrow, and always. Amen.

# CHAPTER TWO

# Owning Up to Our Greatest Obligations: Death and Taxes

## Call to Worship: Psalm 49:5-9

Why should I fear in times of trouble,
  when the iniquity of my persecutors surrounds me,
**Those who trust in their wealth**
  **and boast of the abundance of their riches?**
Truly, no ransom avails for one's life,
  there is no price one can give to God for it.
*All:* **For the ransom of life is costly,**
    **and can never suffice that one should live on forever**
    **and never see the grave.**

# PASTORAL PRAYER

O God of Grace and Mercy, we gather today as your people. As we assemble ourselves, we do so as a people that you have called forth. You, God of Benevolence, have claimed us from our birth and named us at our baptism. Therefore, we and all we have are yours. You are our source, our redeemer, our sustainer, our shepherd. From the baptismal font you have said over all of us, "Thou are my beloved." When we have trouble being the people you have called us to be, help us to remember that we were bought with a price. Help us then give of ourselves and of our possessions by being faithful followers. Only through your promise to us can we say with confidence that we are the sheep of your pasture. You have claimed us as your own, O God. As you give yourself to us, let us give ourselves to you.

Show us the path that leads to you, Lord. Let us pledge our allegiance to your kingdom today. Allow us the privilege of serving in your realm and acknowledge you as our supreme ruler. Give us the wisdom to discern what belongs to you. May we thereby handle the things of your creation with fear and trembling. Make us the people that you envisioned us to be when you fashioned us from the dust of the earth. Help give us a faith that equips us to share the name of Jesus Christ to a world in search of proper authority. And may we, like those who heard Jesus, be amazed at his wise teaching. We pray this and everything in the name of the Lord of all, Jesus Christ. Amen.

# OFFERTORY PRAYER

O Lord, giver of every good gift, help us take to heart Jesus' words when he commanded the leaders of the synagogue: "Give therefore to the emperor the things that are the emperor's, and to God the things that are God's." Make us mindful that all that we are and all that we have, we place at your disposal. May these gifts be gifts that scatter the good news like seed into the world. Make us those who plant the seeds of joy and mercy in all the places we go and bless our gifts that this might be so. We pray this in the name of Jesus. Amen.

# SCRIPTURE: Matthew 22:15-22

# SERMON BRIEF: DEATH AND TAXES

There is a story about an Internal Revenue Service agent who made a phone call to the county-seat town's best-known pastor: "Mr. Bob Smith put down on his tax return that he made a contribution of $3,000 to your church last year. Is that true?" After a brief pause on the other end of the line, the pastor quietly responded, "If he didn't, he will." The familiar adage goes that the two things one cannot escape are death and taxes. Today, we are going to look at what, to some, is the more frightening of the two—taxes.

In this text, Jesus is confronted with a question concerning the head tax paid to the Romans. The Pharisees use false flattery in an attempt to disarm Jesus so that they then can entrap and humiliate him with a tricky yes or no question.

In Jesus' day, questioning the tax system was dangerous business. The establishment of this tax had provoked a revolt by the Jews in the year 6 CE. The Jews had become enraged concerning the placing of God's land at the service of pagans.

Jesus set his own trap for the Pharisees by asking to see the coin used to pay the tax. By doing this, Jesus reminds the Pharisees that they already acknowledge Caesar's authority by having his money in their possession. They possess a Roman coin, bearing the image of emperor and conveying Roman ideology.

## I. We Have a Legitimate Obligation to the State

Jesus simply and profoundly declares that Caesar is owed what bears his image and name—money. Jesus is not drawn into a debate between church and state. He acknowledges that being a servant of God does not exempt you from being a tax-paying servant of the state. Jesus emphasizes, however, that the higher duty is to be rendered to God.

7

## II. We Have a Greater Obligation to God

God, Caesar's Lord, is to be rendered the things that are God's. God is owed what bears his image and name—our very lives.

There is a lovely estate in Georgia, the beautiful grounds of which were being expertly tended by a caretaker. Every tree was trimmed, the grass was mowed, and stately beds of flowers were in bloom. Yet not one soul was around to observe any of the beauty except for the caretaker himself. A visitor surprised the man after stopping to see the striking sight and asked, "When was the owner last here?"

"Oh, ten or twelve years ago, I guess," said the caretaker.

"Then from whom do you get your instructions?"

"From the agent who lives in Atlanta," the caretaker replied.

"Does *he* ever come around to inspect the place?"

"No, can't say that he does," answered the caretaker.

"And yet you keep it trimmed as if he were going to come tomorrow?"

And with that the gardener interrupted the curious visitor: "As if he were going to be here today!"

God calls us to be good stewards of all with which we have been entrusted. One day the Master will come back to check on things—you can count on it. Will God find you and me ready?

Waiting patiently at the cash register, Uncle Sam stands ready to receive a seemingly ever-increasing portion of the money we spend. It's as inevitable as death. The next time you see tax figured into a bill, as you sign the receipt for the credit transaction, remember the words of the penniless itinerant preacher, "Render to Caesar what is Caesar's and to God what is God's." (*Scott Salsman*)

# CHAPTER THREE

# MAKE A DIFFERENCE: BE THE BODY OF CHRIST

## INVOCATION

O Lord, as we worship you this day give us our marching orders that we may fulfill the mission you have given us as a people of God. Make us ever mindful that we, your holy church, are the people called the "Body of Christ." As the body of Christ, like the eucharistic bread, may we too be broken for the world. Help us understand that as part of our calling and mission, we are to be stewards of the gifts and talents that you have entrusted to us. May you say about us as you did your faithful servants: "Well done, good and trustworthy slave(s); you have been trustworthy in a few things, I will put you in charge of many things; enter into the joy of your master" (Matthew 25:21). Amen.

# PASTORAL PRAYER

O God Almighty, save us from a generation that can only see life in terms of individual agendas and through the lens of our modern question: "What is in it for me?" Remind us, O God, that you have given us a community of faith and this community is like family to us. We are a family because, as Paul has written, "In the one Spirit we were all baptized into one body—Jews or Greeks, slaves or free—and we were all made to drink of one Spirit" (1 Corinthians 12:13).

Remind us that we are stronger together than we can ever be as free agents acting upon our own impulses and by our own inclination. Remind us, O Lord of Power, that together we are strong, for where "two or three are gathered" in Jesus' name, then the Christ stands with us. Help us see the biblical wisdom that in staying close to Jesus we may draw from his strength.

Lord of All, we confess that too often the world seduces us by breaking us apart and distracting us from our true household—the household of faith. Help give us the spirit of cooperation that allows us to cleave to one another. May your spirit continue to make us strong in the faith and mindful of the strength we draw from one another, in Christ's name we pray. Amen.

# PRAYER OF CONFESSION

Gracious God, you have created us in a spirit of unity just as your holy being is unified in the Godhead—Creator, Redeemer, Sustainer. We are because you were, and are, and will be. Yet, we have made a mess out of the beauty of your creation, we whom you created as "a little lower than God, / and crowned...with glory and honor" (Psalm 8:5). We trust our fellow creatures too little. We insist on our own way and fail to heed the voices of those who challenge our vision or our agenda. We repent of our sin of pride and inattention to others.

Despite our self-concern and our inclination to protect our turf, help us regard Paul's convincing voice. Paul reminded the

Corinthian church then, as he reminds the church now: "there are many members, yet one body." Help us recognize the wisdom that in Christ all things hang together. Bring to our collective consciousness that we are the body of Christ. Unify us in the spirit of Christ where we have sown seeds of disunity. Bind us to you and to one another in the spirit that will not only announce the good news to our world, but will embody it as well. For our sin of disorder we beg your forgiveness. Speak to us once again. May we together submit to all things in Christ who strengthens us. We pray this in Jesus' name. Amen.

## WORDS OF ASSURANCE

Remember the declaration of our Lord, Jesus the Christ: "Come to me, all you that are weary and are carrying heavy burdens, and I will give you rest. Take my yoke upon you, and learn from me; for I am gentle and humble in heart, and you will find rest for your souls. For my yoke is easy, and my burden is light" (Matthew 11:28-30). Give us the courage to be Christ for one another.

## SCRIPTURE: 1 Corinthians 12:12-31a

## SERMON BRIEF: COOPERATION THAT MAKES A DIFFERENCE

A discovery has been made that when the roots of trees touch, there is a substance present that reduces competition. This unknown fungus helps link roots of various trees, including dissimilar species. A whole forest may be incorporated together in this manner. If one tree has access to nutrients, another to water, and a third to sunlight, the trees have the means to cooperate with one another to live.

Multiple analyses can be made to show a need for cooperation and support for one another. The tree illustration is one way to analyze the situation, while Paul offers another in his letter to the Corinthians, using the body as a symbol of cooperation.

# I. Cooperation with the Head: Christ (vv. 12-13)

Paul pictures Jesus in the Corinthian text as the head of the church. Christ is the unifying power that keeps the body together. In this role he helps, thinks, guides, and directs the entire body.

A university professor performed an experiment in his classes that awed him every time he did it. On an oak table he placed a pile of horseshoe nails and in one corner of the same room was a powerful dynamo. When the electric current was flipped on and the poles of the battery were brought up under the table, immediately there was constituted about the table a field of magnetic force. As long as the field of force was maintained the loose horseshoe nails could be built up into various forms, like a cube, a square, or an arch. As long as the current was on, the nails would stay in exactly the form placed as if they had been soldered together. But the moment the current was cut off the nails would fall into a shapeless mass.

Christ's unifying power is to Christians as the field of magnetic force was to the nails. If we do not allow him to be the head of life or the church, there will be a great collapse of morals, ethics, and spirit.

# II. Cooperation with the Body: Church (vv. 14-27)

As Christ is the example of cooperation with God for individuals, he is also an example for the rest of the body. On a blank leaf of a grandmother's Bible was drawn a circle with several radii converging at the center, which was named Christ. On the radii were written the names of different Christian denominations. Underneath the circle she had written, "The nearer the center, the nearer to one another." Today, we need to be nearer the center!

## III. Cooperation with a Purpose: Service (vv. 28-31a)

Paul teaches that each Christian has a distinct contribution to give for the benefit of the whole. It comes by way of service to others. In his treatise on Christian liberty, Martin Luther said, "A Christian man is the most free lord of all, and subject to none; a Christian man is the most dutiful servant of all, and subject to every one." Christ has demonstrated with certainty that serving others is the Christian's responsibility. *(Derl G. Keefer)*

# CHAPTER FOUR

# WHO NEEDS BIGGER BARNS?

## CALL TO WORSHIP:
### from 2 Corinthians 12:8-10

Paul wrote: "Three times I appealed to the Lord about this [thorn]."
**The Lord said to Paul: "My grace is sufficient for you, for power is made perfect in weakness."**
So, we will boast all the more gladly of our weaknesses, so that the power of Christ may dwell in us.
**Therefore we are content with weaknesses, insults, hardships, persecutions, and calamities for the sake of Christ;**
*All:* **For whenever we are weak, then we are strong.**

## PRAYER OF CONFESSION

Forgive us, O Lord, for we have been deceived by our world into thinking that it is by our own merit and work that we secure our own future. We confess that too often we desire to have more, often at the expense of others. We have been subjected to a host of modern marketers that tell us again and again that their products will free us from whatever ails us. Yet, purchase after purchase has only proved that our world only offers us mirages to quench the deeper thirst we experience as human beings. Remind us again that it is you, O Lord, who offers to us the eternal truth found in creation's beauty and sparkle. Give us once again that courage that can say no to the world and its lure. Grant us the serenity that comes from living in your abundance. May we once again turn to you for security and a life truly worth living. Help us repent of our penchant for being defrauded of authentic life and help us turn God-ward—yet once again— today. In the name of our Messiah we pray. Amen.

## WORDS OF ASSURANCE

The book of Hebrews tells us that "faith is the assurance of things hoped for, the conviction of things not seen" (Hebrews 11:1). Remember that Jesus told us that we were the light of Christ and the salt of the earth. Christ assures us that we have the name "Christ bearer." May we so believe where we have not seen, that in bearing Christ's light, we may be worthy of that name. Amen.

## OFFERTORY PRAYER

God, you have given to us without measure; now let us give unto your realm without measure as well. As we do, burn into our hearts the words that Jesus said: "It is more blessed to give than to receive" (Acts 20:35).

## SCRIPTURE: Luke 12:13-21

## SERMON BRIEF: WHO NEEDS BIGGER BARNS?

Madeline was going to her college reunion. It would be the first time she would see her former classmates since graduation day, and she was anxious about the event. "What can I say about myself " she asked. "I've read the alumni news column in the college magazine, with all the success stories. And look at me; I've put on a lot of weight in the last ten years. I didn't get a job in my chosen field. At the moment I'm not even employed. How could I be, with two toddlers at home?"

Madeline worried that she would be considered a failure, compared to classmates whose lives seemed more glamorous and affluent. Her former roommate reassured her that on the contrary, many would admire her; she had a devoted husband and healthy, lovable children. She was a good mother, a leader among the laity at church, and had plans to further her education once her daughters were older. Yet Madeline knew that a college reunion could be a "day of reckoning" of sorts. She was taking stock of her life and wondering how she would be judged.

## I. Bigger Barns Indicate Spiritual Myopia

If Madeline was overconcerned with human opinion rather than God's, the "rich fool" of the parable was concerned with no one's opinion save his own. His only point of reference was himself—his crops, his barns, his pleasure, his supposedly unlimited future. As the center of his own universe, he gave no thought to ethical responsibility toward others or accountability to God.

In *Habits of the Heart*, Robert Bellah described such an attitude as "Sheilaism." Sheila was a woman in one of Bellah's case studies who acknowledged no external point of reference in spiritual or moral matters. She believed in "my own little voice...just try to love yourself and be gentle with yourself. You know, I guess, take care of each other." Sheila thought she was a religious, ethical person if she adhered to these internal (and entirely subjective) principles. There was no point of reckoning outside herself, no judgment from a righteous and holy God.

The bigger barns built by the rich fool and the Sheilaism practiced by so many people today indicate spiritual myopia: failure to think beyond today and oneself. Such people may lay up treasure for themselves, but they are not rich toward God, and the consequences are grim.

## II. Look to the Lord of the Harvest, Not Bigger Barns

Jesus says that a person's life does not consist in the abundance of possessions. We might add that it also does not consist of an abundance of accomplishments, applause, or self-indulgence. All that we are and have ultimately belongs to God, and as stewards, we will have to give God an accounting of the use of our time and gifts and energy.

Unlike a class reunion, we have no idea when the Lord will take stock of what we have done with our lives. But it will happen to every one of us. It may be tonight. It may not be for years. To be "rich toward God," Christians must learn to think of themselves as laborers in the Master's fields, rather than private landowners answerable to no one. The harvest is Christ's, not ours, and our Lord calls us to use the resources at our disposal to help others and thus glorify him. (*Carol M. Norén*)

CHAPTER FIVE

# PLAYING *THE* PRICE *IS* RIGHT

## INVOCATION

O Sovereign, Eternal and Everlasting, inspire our hearts and lives with the words of life offered us this day as we worship you. In Christ, O God, the eternal meets the temporal and we see what a person looks like who dwells in perfect harmony with you. In Jesus' baptism he submitted to your eternal authority over life and death and even beyond—in your resurrection of Christ. During holy worship today furnish us a foretaste of your Divine Realm and make us ever eager to commit ourselves to your plan for our world. In Christ we have seen your heavenly presence. Help us validate our lives by the pattern that Christ presents. As a united people of Christ, we pray in Jesus' holy name and for his sake. Amen.

## PRAYER OF CONFESSION

God of Mercy, we who take an honest look at our lives know full well that we have not lived up to the standard that you set for us as Bible-believers, nor as creatures fashioned in your divine imagination. Too often we have chased the strategy of our own flawed imagination. We confess that we have traded our birthright, like Esau, for a mess of pottage. Of course, our pottage is not a stew cooked in the wilderness. Instead we concoct our stew by whatever up-to-the-minute fad that confers on us the moniker of "those sophisticates in the know." Help us reacquaint ourselves with the weighty truth of Scripture and the grand narrative of faith. Help us recognize the sage and ancient wisdom contained in the stories of both saints and sinners supplied for us in the stories of our Israelite and Christian forebears. Make us appreciate that we do not create a moral or righteous society. Rather you have created a world of shalom that we merely mirror by lives dedicated to your peace, O God, which passes all human understanding.

Forgive us we pray. Inspire in us a community of Jesus that embraces unity, rather than division, humility rather than pride. Give us a sense of your original vision for your blessed creation and help us carve out our place in it. We cannot do this by our own power, but only in the power that Jesus offers us through the Holy Spirit. It is in the holy name of Jesus that we pray. Amen.

## WORDS OF ASSURANCE

God does not deal with us according to our sins, nor repay us according to our iniquities. For as the heavens are high above the earth, so great is God's steadfast love toward those who fear him; as far as the east is from the west, so far God removes our transgressions from us. As God has demonstrated his loyalty to us by sending his Son for our salvation, let us show our loyalty to God by being a faithful and compassionate people (see Psalm 103:10-13).

## PRAYER BEFORE THE READING OF HOLY SCRIPTURE

O God, Author of Everlasting Life, as we open your Holy Word, may it be for us like wilderness manna. Let it inspire us with the power of your Holy Spirit as it satisfies the hunger of our souls and makes us a people worthy of the name "Christian." May your word inspire us to once again claim to be your people in this world as we enact the drama of salvation. Amen.

# SCRIPTURE: Luke 12:49-56

# SERMON BRIEF: THE PRICE IS RIGHT

*The Price Is Right* is a very popular television program. The host invites selected contestants to name their prices for specific items. The person who chooses the correct amount or suggests the amount closest to the actual amount is declared the winner. It is an exciting game show with each player being coached with prices from the audience. Participants and viewers alike get caught up in selecting the price that is right.

In the biblical text, Jesus continues to challenge his followers to consider the price in following him. To be a follower of Christ is not as easy as a walk in the park or a casual stroll down memory lane. It is difficult, and the text speaks with sharp realism of the cost of commitment to Jesus.

## The Cost of Distress (vv. 49-50)

Salvation begins with an awareness of the distress of one's life. Simply put, a person without Christ as personal Savior is separated from God.

When Jesus spoke of fire, he was speaking of judgment. Fire in Jewish thought is usually a symbol of judgment. As he was speaking of the coming kingdom of God, he viewed its beginning as a time of God's judgment upon the people. Some Jewish leaders of his era believed that the criterion of their judgment was different from all others. Their being descendants of Abraham was qualification enough to "pass through the fire."

Many today place their hope of acceptance by God on a birth certificate, membership in the *correct* church, humanitarian efforts, or squeaky-clean morality. Jesus addresses this mindset with the declaration that he has come to be the divining rod with his hot words about fire.

Verse 50 gives us a glimpse into the Savior's heart as he already looks toward Calvary and death. Having been baptized by John in the Jordan, the baptism of which he now speaks is his coming death. Gethsemane is already present in his thoughts. His commitment to the Lord is evident in the tone of distress. In declaring one's faithful intent to walk the walk of Jesus, we should not be surprised when we must pay the cost of distress.

## II. The Cost of Division (vv. 51-53)

Each of the three Synoptic Gospels records Jesus' explanation regarding the division in families that would occur because of loyalty to him. Ultimate loyalty to Christ moves all other relationships, even family, to a secondary position. People will divide over what costs are to be paid in being loyal to him.

Although families may be divided over Christ, no family ties are stronger than those in Christ. Human history continues to demonstrate the multiplicity of reasons we have chosen to be divided in him. Ultimately, the entire human race is divided over Jesus. Some are walking the narrow way to life eternal, while many are walking the broad way to eternal death.

## III. The Cost of Discernment (vv. 54-56)

Palestinian Jews did not have to watch the Weather Channel to be able to anticipate the weather. Clouds forming to the west over the Mediterranean Sea meant that they could expect rain. When they felt the hot breeze from the desert south begin to blow on their faces, they knew that the dreaded *sirocco* wind would come soon with its blazing heat.

Jesus rebuked his listeners stating that, while they were very wise in discerning the signs of the weather—physical signs—they were ignorant in reading the spiritual signs all around them. The signs of their times pointed to the Messiah with the arrival of his kingdom. They had eyes to see and ears to hear, but they chose to be blind and deaf.

Today, signs of spiritual awakening are all around us. Those who see them take off their shoes, recognizing they stand on holy ground. The rest, in the words of Elizabeth Barrett Browning, "...sit round it, and pluck blackberries...!"

Jesus said with his words and his life that "the price is right" for the cost of discipleship. The question is: are we willing to pay the price? (*John Lee Taylor*)

CHAPTER SIX

# COUNTING THE COST MEANS QUALITY NOT QUANTITY

## PRAYER TO BEGIN WORSHIP

O Lord, Holy and Righteous God, as we come into the realm of this sacred sanctuary and its hallowed space, may we defer to your awesome character. It is you who formed us from the dust and it is to the dust that we shall return. While we are here on your verdant earth, let us be good stewards of the time you have granted us as stewards of your holy mystery. Make us a people who embrace Micah's injunction: "to do justice, and to love kindness, and to walk humbly with your God" (Micah 6:8). Help us meet the demands of our lives with devotion to you. Grant us courage to live with joyful obedience such that we may harvest an inheritance of eternal life. In Jesus' name we pray. Amen.

## PRAYER OF CONFESSION

O God, our Heavenly Creator, we confess that we have lost our way. Too easily we are distracted from what really matters. In our better moments we recognize that life is better than death and love is superior to hate. Yet, far too often in the heat of the moment, we lose our heads—and perhaps worse—we lose our hearts. We do things and say things that betray our lack of faith and perhaps even our lack of emotional control. We each strive to control our life. We strive to make a name for ourselves. We make every effort to protect our loved ones and ourselves. We are well meaning, Lord, but sometimes we choose paths that lead us away from you. So today we acknowledge our sin and confess our shortcomings, and with humility we ask you to help us strive for the greater gifts and to show us a still more excellent way.

We want to be your people, but we are sometimes afraid of your demands. Our fears run deep and we cannot overcome them by ourselves. You know, O Lord, that we have tried. Remind us once again that the beginning of wisdom is to trust your holiness. Help us cling to this trust and live with the faith that you will provide for us. As we worship you in deep conviction, speak the words of comfort and hope to us once again. Empower us with the Holy Spirit that we may say with the Gospel writer, "I believe; help my unbelief" (Mark 9:24).

## WORDS OF ASSURANCE

The Lord of the Universe assures us that in our human lives before God we are to "first sit down and estimate the cost." Be assured that our greatest possession—the only possession that we can never lose—is our possession of you, O God. We are God's people. It is God who made us and we are God's. "We are God's people and the sheep of God's pasture" (see Psalm 100:3). Thanks be to God. Amen.

## OFFERTORY PRAYER

O God, we bring to you this day only that which you have first graciously entrusted to us. We dedicate these offerings for gospel work in this world that you created and have deemed to share with us. Bless those who receive and those who give these gifts. Amen.

## SCRIPTURE: Luke 14:25-33

## SERMON BRIEF: COUNT THE COST

One of the remarkable characteristics of our Lord was his insistence that those who follow him realize the cost. There was no diluting what it meant to accept him as Lord of life. In Jesus' challenge to follow, he underscored with red and highlighted in bright color the hardships involved. His appeal for disciples was primarily directed to the few who would follow, not to the generalized multitudes. His concern was in quality, not quantity. How refreshing, for in many areas of Christendom today the opposite is true!

### I. The Demand (v. 25)

According to the text, "many multitudes" went with him. The word *went* means "to go along with." There were great numbers of people who were "going along" with him, following on the basis of a mixed bag of motives. Some were sincere. Some were curious. Some were willing to enlist in the army of anyone who might "restore the kingdom to Israel." The multitude felt no requirements and no demands in following the Messiah.

In an instant, Jesus burst their bubble of ease. He was on the way to Jerusalem. They thought he was on his way to worldly power, and they wanted to be a part of it. These messianic groupies had to make a decision: Would they be camp followers or devoted disciples?

### II. The Devotion (v. 26)

In the vivid vocabulary of this ancient culture, Jesus says that those who would follow him must have a love for him that causes other loves to shrink in comparison. The strong word *hate* grates on our sensitivity. There were several meanings of this word in the day of Jesus. I believe the most applicable in Christ's usage is this: compared to one's devotion to Christ, all other devotions on any human level become secondary. Even one's life must become subjugated to Jesus as one of his disciples. And *life* means one's complete self.

Devotion to Jesus as one of his disciples means that there is absolutely nothing that comes between the follower and Jesus.

## III. The Death (v. 27)

Taking up one's cross means death to self rather than denial of self. The cross is an instrument of execution ending in death. Today, in our modern Christianity, we have equated the cross more with service than with sacrifice. Those who heard these startling words of Jesus knew without doubt that he was speaking of death. With no uncertainty, Jesus is calling the people to follow him even unto their deaths.

## IV. The Dimensions (vv. 28-33)

In defining further the cost of discipleship, Jesus uses two parables as illustrations. The first is a builder who prepares to build a tower. The second is a warrior who prepares to go to battle. In each, the emphasis is on counting the cost.

The tower was probably to be constructed on the farm to protect crops and vineyards from animals that would destroy and from people who would steal. The intent was a positive one. What would be detrimental was to begin the building and not finish it. Beginning without adequate finances would cause derision and shame from neighbors. Such a monument to bad planning would stand as a poor witness to the builder's ability to finish what he had begun. Jesus is focusing on the end of one's journey with him as well as the beginning.

The warrior king wisely counted how many troops he had before going into battle with his enemy. With ten thousand men, how victorious could he be against an army of twenty thousand commanded by his enemy? Having counted the cost, he came to the conclusion that the better part of wisdom was not to go to war. He sought peace without the risk of battle. Jesus' point in the parable was the necessity of counting the cost before enlisting in his army.

Verse 33 sums up this section with a call to "forsake all." Are we willing to give up all that we are and all that we have to serve Christ? His call is for a willingness to surrender everything that would impede one's total commitment to him. *(John Lee Taylor)*

---

# Chapter Seven

# Why God Doesn't Want Your Money

## Invocation

We praise and magnify your holy name, O Lord. You are our righteousness. You have been our rock and an ever-present help in time of our need. As we worship today, tell us again once again that you and you alone are God. You have nourished us at your banquet table and taught us the way to abundant life. In your grace there is mercy and forgiveness of sin. If we would but cling to you and your instruction for us, then we would live lives that endure to the very end of time. Send your Holy Spirit upon us to give us a vision of the heavenly places so that we can minister to those who share this mundane world with us. May we look upon all persons as sisters and brothers for whom Christ died. Open our hearts and our mouths and we shall show forth praise. Amen.

## Prayer of Confession

O Lord, we confess that too often we get caught up in the trappings of religion. Too easily we get caught up in what we do for the church and how much money we give. Help us put aside our hypocrisy and live with joyful, thankful hearts. Help us live as

Jesus showed us. Yet Lord, when we measure ourselves against Jesus' injunction "Be perfect, therefore, as your heavenly Father is perfect" (Matthew 5:48), then who can stand? Or when Jesus tells the young ruler, "If you wish to be perfect, go, sell your possessions, and give the money to the poor, and you will have treasure in heaven; then come, follow me" (Matthew 19:21), then what are we to do? We know we cannot be perfect and we have many possessions. Yet, you have told us "strive first for the kingdom of God and his righteousness, and all these things will be given to you as well" (Matthew 6:33). Help us see that in our thirst for your righteousness we will find the perfection that you seek. We cannot do it in our own strength, but rather in the strength of your mighty hand and outstretched arm. We regularly fail to remember that you came to search for those who are lost and to salvage the lives of those perishing. For while we strive for perfection, assure us that we find our real perfection in you. Heal us of our sin. We pray this and all things in the powerful name of Jesus. Amen.

## WORDS OF ASSURANCE: Isaiah 1:16-17

Our God has commanded us to:

"Wash yourselves; make yourselves clean;
   remove the evil of your doings
   from before my eyes;
cease to do evil,
   learn to do good;
seek justice,
   rescue the oppressed,
defend the orphan,
   plead for the widow"

The Lord has put within our hearts a spirit of truth and holiness. Embrace that spirit as the forgiven and redeemed people of God. Amen.

# PRAYER BEFORE THE READING OF HOLY SCRIPTURE

Lord, attune our ears to the reading of your Holy Word. Grant to us a new hearing of these texts, so that they may speak to us the Word afresh. In hearing this word, then make us disciples with a passion for the Word that comes from you. Amen.

# SCRIPTURE: Isaiah 1:10-18

# SERMON BRIEF: WHY GOD DOESN'T WANT YOUR MONEY

Every Sunday she sat in the pew, rarely missing worship. With a somewhat dramatic flair, she would place her offering envelope in the plate as it passed each week. She was also one of the most bitter persons I have ever known. She was unyielding in business, blaming in relationships, and bitter about the past.

Isaiah gives a word of warning to us whenever we fail to integrate faith and life: "Bringing offerings is futile; incense is an abomination to me. New moon and sabbath and calling of convocation—I cannot endure solemn assemblies with iniquity" (v. 13).

## I. God Does Not Call Us to Be Religious; God Calls Us to Be Faithful

Today's text points to the immorality of insincere worship. The hypocrisy of religious practice separated from faithful living has far-reaching effects. We fail to nurture our soul when we fail to integrate worship with holy living. Further, such hypocrisy does untold damage to the Christian witness. Such "solemn assemblies with iniquity" are not what God desires in true worship.

Christianity is a lifestyle of discipleship, not a religion of empty piety. We are all sinners in need of grace. None of us are made righteous by occupying a pew. It is what we bring to worship as well as what we take from worship that leads to a healthy soul. We bring our brokenness and our need for forgiveness. We leave with hope, grace, and the power of God's Spirit to act out our faith.

## II. Faith without Action Is Hollow

Doctrine and deed dare not be separated. Worship divorced from the practice of our faith misses the mark. We worship the God revealed through Christ. It is the same Christ who walked among the hurt and outcast, surrendered personal comfort for human need, and offered himself so that God's grace would be revealed. This is a Christ of both word and deed.

Through Isaiah, we hear what God requires of true worship. We are to "learn to do good; seek justice, rescue the oppressed, defend the orphan, plead for the widow" (v. 17). It is a reminder that God's dominion is wonderfully different. The kingdom of God is a place where the impotent are given power, the victims are given justice, and the desperate are given hope.

## III. God's Power to Forgive and to Heal

The true worship of God requires an open heart and a willing spirit. These are essential to accepting God's grace. We do not bring gifts in order to buy grace, prove our faith, or boast about the level of our stewardship. We offer our prayers, presence, gifts, and service as an act of devotion.

Only those broken by sin and the hurts of this world can truly appreciate the power of forgiveness. God's mercy and grace break down barriers, heal our hurts, mend our minds, and pardon our past. Such is the nature of a God whose ways are not our ways. Through the prophet, God speaks a word of grace to those of Isaiah's day, and to us today. It is not an appeal for gifts and service offered with insincere piety, it is an appeal for our very souls. It is an appeal that comes with a gift of grace. "Come now, let us argue it out, says the LORD: though your sins are like scarlet, they shall be like snow, though they are red like crimson, they shall become like wool" (v. 18). (*Gary G. Kindley*)

# CHAPTER EIGHT

# WHAT GOD DESERVES

## CALL TO WORSHIP: Psalm 92:1-5a, 12-15a

It is good to give thanks to the LORD,
   to sing praises to your name, O Most High;
**To declare your steadfast love in the morning
   and your faithfulness by night.**
For you, O LORD, have made me glad by your work;
   at the works of your hands I sing for joy.
**How great are your works, O LORD!**
The righteous flourish like the palm tree,
   and grow like a cedar in Lebanon.
**They are planted in the house of the LORD;
   they flourish in the courts of our God.**
In old age they still produce fruit;
   they are always green and full of sap,
**All: Showing that the LORD is upright;
   [God] is my rock.**

## PRAYER OF CONFESSION

God of Grace and God of Grandeur, we confess that we have difficulty in reckoning our duty to our nation and to you. We love our nation and try to be good citizens of this temporal realm. Yet, often we partition our loyalties. We confound our own minds. We habitually believe that we must choose between the love of country and our allegiance to you. Remind us of Paul's truth when he wrote the church at Rome, "Let every person be subject to the governing authorities; for there is no authority except from God, and those authorities that exist have been instituted by God" (Romans 13:1).

The truth is that we have attempted to separate our world into what belongs to us and what belongs to you, O God. In our honest moments, when we take our story of faith seriously, we must confess with Paul "there is no authority except from God." Therefore, help us work in the course of our worldly processes of state affairs to bring your word and authority to bear on our daily lives. Help us remember that what you require of us is simply "to do justice, and to love kindness, and to walk humbly with your God" (Micah 6:8). As a sincere gesture of our request for your divine mercy, Gracious Lord, may Micah's words become a compass for our lives. Let us be those who dedicate ourselves to the life you created for us—and may we spread the joy of the good news to all persons with justice and equity. We pray this in the name of the greatest liberator of all, Jesus Christ. Amen.

## WORDS OF ASSURANCE

"Who is a God like you, pardoning iniquity and passing over the transgression of the remnant of your possession? God does not retain his anger forever, because God delights in showing clemency. The Lord will again have compassion upon us; God will tread our iniquities under foot. You [O Lord] will cast all our sins into the depths of the sea" (see Micah 7:18-19).

## OFFERTORY PRAYER

God of Grace and God of Glory, we ask you to bless both the giver of these gifts, as well as those who receive them. May we be mindful of the source of all gifts given in Jesus' name. Whether these gifts are great or minute, may they symbolize our deep attachment to you and your realm. Amen.

# PASTORAL PRAYER

Almighty God, we gather as your people who live in hope. Our lives provide us many opportunities to speak words of peace and reconciliation, but often we have not the daring. Make us bold not only to speak your word but also to live it. In order to live in the fullness of the gospel, remind us that it is by grace that we live and die. Help us confess our sin and open us to the new life that only the gospel of Jesus Christ affords.

Help us in this hour of worship offer to you, O God, our sacrifices of praise and thanksgiving. Make us a people who are so thoroughly grateful for the life you offer us that we become worthy stewards in the household of faith. Grant to us a generosity that captured the hearts and lives of those first disciples who formed and expanded your church to the ends of the earth.

Lord, you know we often want to take the easy way out. Too often it just seems easier not to say anything than to get involved. We confess that by not standing in righteousness with you, we allow evil, sin, and destruction to run over other people even those closest to us. Forgive us Lord. Be our standard and grant us the endurance to be your standard-bearers in this community.

As we pray today, help us remember those in our neighborhood, our state, our country, our world who need your assurance and grace. Wherever possible let us reach out to others with both words and deeds. Enable us to offer grace and mercy in your name. All this we ask in Christ's holy name. Amen.

# SCRIPTURE: Matthew 22:15-22

# SERMON BRIEF: WHAT GOD DESERVES

We sometimes think we are so smart that we have a better plan than the Almighty. Rationalization is not reality, and flawed reason only leads to phony redemption. It happened in Jesus' day, it still happens today, and it still does not work. The Pharisees tried to entrap Jesus. They were looking for an easy out—a way to rid themselves of this troubling rabbi who spoke of God on personal terms. They asked him a question that would put the law of Caesar in tension with the law of God.

What they did not understand, and many still do not, is that God wants commitment rather than compromise. God is out to save our souls, not pick our pockets or squabble about petty religion. Christ calls us to give to God what God rightly deserves.

## I. God Is Worthy of Our Worship

Give to God the things that are God's due. The Divine merits our loyalty, our praise, our celebration of life and God's creation. God is not concerned with the legalism of our religious practice or whether we gave 10 percent of our paycheck to the last decimal place. God desires our complete commitment: body, mind, and soul. The Gospels remind us that discipleship is not a halfway proposition. The apostles "left everything, and followed Jesus" (Luke 5:11 GNT). Jesus Christ is Lord over all of life. The cross and the empty tomb are real and are worthy of a faith response that is equally genuine. We give, live, serve, and pray because an incredibly gracious gift has been given to us. Anything we do is but a response to what God has done.

## II. God Is Uplifted in Our Service

Christians are persons who have answered the call to serve God. Those who desire to follow Christ must proclaim God's love by their living, giving, serving, and praying. No matter how tough the journey gets, there is almost certainly someone whose struggle is greater.

A man's wife falls deep into the dark abyss of Alzheimer's. The blank expression, disassociation of thought, and purposeless movement characterize her plight. Lovingly he cares for her, bathes her, brushes her hair, as she falls deeper and deeper away from reality. When she becomes bedfast, he cares for her round-the-clock. His own life is absorbed by her care, and he has little time for personal diversion. No greater witness to Christian marriage exists than the complete sacrifice of one's life for the love of another. By his service, love is uplifted and God is honored.

## III. God Is Honored in Our Relationships

You cannot sincerely worship God and be unkind to God's creation. There is no integrity in being a cross-wearer if you cannot be a cross-bearer. Life and relationships are tough. Marriage, parenting, and career all have their challenges. Christian persons persevere throughout life's journey and strive to remain faithful, loving, and kind in their relationships.

There was a successful chaplain who seemed to have it all. He was respected by his peers, honored for his service, and promoted for his successes. It was all a hollow reality, for his marriage was in shambles and his temper would lash out at those closest to him, his family. Confronted by his pastor, he was asked three questions: "How do your peers rate you?" "How do you rate yourself?" and "How does God measure your success?" He knew he was successful in the eyes of his peers, and his career helped him put his self-assessment on top. He had not truly thought about God's criteria for success.

His pastor answered for him, "If you cannot love and serve those closest to you and be worthy of their respect, you do not love God." God requires justice, kindness, and humility in relationships. God offers abundant living when we realize that success is not measured by the world's standards but by God's standard. (*Gary G. Kindley*)

# CHAPTER NINE

# RISKING TO MAKE THE RIGHT INVESTMENT

## OPENING PRAYER

May the sound of our prayers, holy songs, and understanding of scripture be pleasing in your sight, O God. Let our worship equip us for holy living. As we assemble to examine our lives through the lens of your holy will, may we be true to our calling in Jesus Christ in whose name we pray. Amen.

## PRAYER OF CONFESSION

Benevolent God, we want to be wise investors; yet we confess that too often we invest our time, our talent, and our money foolishly. We invest in things thinking that things will give us security. When we come to worship we are reminded that Jesus came to give us abundant life, not to give us more stuff. In our better moments we know that stuff does not lead to eternal life; only a relationship with Jesus can do that. But we are anxious and foolish people. We confess of our myopic view of seeing the world through the lens of ourselves only. Heal us of our blindness and empower us with your vision of who we are and who we can become. Grant us the grace and courage to walk that narrow path which leads to you.

Give us the courage of our convictions, O Lord of Life. Make us the people that you imagined at creation. Heal our lack of trust so that we may wholly and completely follow you as disciples of the Risen Lord. We genuinely desire to be your hands and feet in the world, so give us the volition to follow our hearts into a deeper relationship with you. Forgive us in all the places that we have fallen short and give us an enduring vision of the realm of God that we desire to serve. Help us learn to invest together and live as the gracious body of Christ in our community. In this and in everything we offer our prayers in the name of the one you sent to be our Messiah, Jesus Christ. Amen.

## WORDS OF ASSURANCE

Hear these words that await faithful disciples, "Well done, good and trustworthy servant; you have been trustworthy in a few things, I will put you in charge of many things; enter into the joy of your master" (see Matthew 25:23). Rest assured that God comforts those who show faith and trust in God's promise. Amen.

## OFFERTORY PRAYER

Blessed are those who can give without remembering; and take without forgetting. Amen.

## SCRIPTURE: Matthew 25:14-30

## SERMON BRIEF: MAKING THE RIGHT INVESTMENT

One of the major news items of the year involved the stock market. I remember when there was speculation about what would happen if the stock market ever reached two thousand. Now it has reached several times that level. Whatever kind of advice you want about the market you will find: some say it's time to invest, while others say it's time to get your money out!

Investing always carries an element of risk. I asked a stockbroker about high, moderate, and low risk investments. He preferred to speak in terms of highly speculative, aggressive, and conservative. Responsible stewardship implies making wise investments. It is interesting that while the Bible tells us to take no thought for tomorrow because we should trust God to take care of us, it also tells us to be responsible stewards.

## I. A Wise Investor

Jesus tells a parable about a wealthy landowner going on a journey and entrusting the management of his estate to his servants. This landowner recognized the different capabilities of each steward, so he gave to each the amount of money that he thought that one could manage—five talents to one, two to another, and one to the third. There is no inherent unfairness or partiality here. It is the judgment of the owner as to how much responsibility each servant could handle.

The effective, or wise, investors were willing to assume the risks of making an investment. They knew this was what their master expected. There was less pressure on them in one sense because it wasn't really their money they were investing. In another sense, there was more pressure because they were managing the account for someone else. The five-talent and the two-talent investors each doubled their investment.

## II. A Foolish Investor

The one-talent investor was afraid of the consequences of making a bad investment, so he took the money and hid it. When the master returns, we get an insight into what lay at the root of the foolish man's reluctance to invest. He had a harsh and inadequate view of his master. He was paralyzed by fear, and took his one talent and buried it in the ground. The foolish investor said to his master, "I know what a hard man you are. You harvest where you haven't sown. You always manage to get the best out of any transaction."

Not only did he underestimate his master's character, he underestimated even his own abilities as an investor. In effect, he said, "You are so shrewd and adept at getting the absolute most out of every investment you make that I couldn't ever begin to measure up to your standards."

## III. The Reaction of the Master

The master was pleased with the wise investors. He said, "Well done. You've been faithful with this little bit of responsibility. I'll give you the opportunity to have more responsibility." To the foolish investor, though, he said, "You wicked and lazy servant." He lost his opportunity ever to do anything again for his master.

What do the investors get for their wise investing? It's questionable whether they got a share of the profits. They did get more responsibility and opportunity. Their reward is to be a larger and more significant part of the master's overall enterprise.

God never promised that we would get rich. God does give us an opportunity to invest our lives in something of eternal significance. To those who invest faithfully and wisely, God says, "Well done." What other pay do you need? (*Mark A. Johnson*)

## BENEDICTION: Numbers 6:24-26

Now go into the world as empowered and equipped disciples.
May the LORD bless you and keep you;
> the LORD make his face to shine upon you,
>> and be gracious to you;
> the LORD lift up his countenance upon you,
>> and give you peace.

# CHAPTER TEN

# THE MIRACLE OF IMMORTAL GIVING

## CALL TO WORSHIP: Psalm 37:3-6, 11, 39-40

Trust in the LORD, and do good;
  so you will live in the land, and enjoy security.
**Take delight in the LORD,**
  **and he will give you the desires of your heart.**
Commit your way to the LORD;
  trust in him, and he will act.
**He will make your vindication shine like the light,**
  **and the justice of your cause like the noonday.**
But the meek shall inherit the land, and delight themselves in
      abundant prosperity.
**The salvation of the righteous is from the LORD;**
  **he is their refuge in the time of trouble.**
**All: The LORD helps them and rescues them;**
      **he rescues them from the wicked, and saves them,**
      **because they take refuge in him.**

# PASTORAL PRAYER

O Lord of Heaven and Earth, because "we have borne the image of the one of dust," may "we also bear the image of the one of heaven" (1 Corinthians 15:49). The greatest gift any of us will ever receive is eternal life that appears in Jesus' resurrection.

Through this powerful moment in divine/human history, you redeemed all of our hours and days. Make us mindful that we are bought with a price and are precious in your sight. When the world beats us up and knocks us down, let us stand on the fact that we are children of the King, the Creator and Sustainer of the universe. Yet, let us not be arrogant or boastful. Remind us that true power begins with kneeling in prayer and listening to you.

As your people, you not only save us from sin and death. You also save us for a life that befits the gospel. Give us the verve to act as disciples and speak boldly the gospel words of truth in love. In Jesus' name we pray. Amen.

# OFFERTORY PRAYER

May these gifts, which we pass along to your storehouse, be gratifying to you, O God of all Grace. Bless these offerings as they are distributed throughout the world to those in need. May these gifts bless the lives of those who receive, even as these gifts bless those who have given them. We ask this in the holy and merciful name of Jesus. Amen.

# SCRIPTURE: 1 Corinthians 15:35-38, 42-50

# SERMON BRIEF: THE IMMORTAL GIFT

In this Scripture text, Paul lays it all down. The resurrected body is of God's doing: the miracle accomplished by God is not only in the gift of new life. It is also in the redemption of the body that receives new life. Crucial to this understanding is the idea that immortality is not given to the finite. The perishable must be transformed into something more, something better. The kingdom shall be inherited but not by those who remain the same. The resurrection miracle continues in the change wrought over us.

"Just As I Am, Without One Plea" has been a favored hymn for generations because it speaks to the joy felt by those who receive the redemptive love of God in Jesus. All persons are invited, regardless of state or position, to come to God through Jesus for salvation. The crucified and resurrected one brings for them an escape from the dread of their existence. They, and we, can be accepted.

"Just as I am" does not mean just as I will stay. The God who redeems us not only moves us from something, but also moves us to something. The expectation is that we will grow into all that God has made us to be. We are no longer enslaved to the old self. The sin of our existence has been cast aside as a matter of imprisonment. We are freed to live in the hope and power of a God who specializes in redemption.

But what should we make of those who claim to follow Jesus? Many claim to follow, but are they different? Flesh and blood cannot inherit the kingdom; that is to say, to be beholden to the vices and trappings of this life is to fail to follow Jesus. Pop music star Madonna sang a song in the 1980s called "Material Girl" that epitomizes all that is perishable, that persons crave in this culture—cars, diamonds, fame, money, power, pleasure. None of these in and of themselves are evil. However, when we become possessed by them we fall victim to "flesh and blood."

We cannot ignore, in our capitalist, economically driven society, the perishable temptations of a Wall Street, Internet, or a "Benjamin" (colloquialism for $100 bills) mad culture. Paul says that there is something more in the reality of resurrection—that the immortal gift through Jesus can become flesh and real.

My daughter Alyssa and her friends repeated this rhyme during the Christmas season years ago: "What shall I give him poor as I am? If I were a shepherd I'd give him a lamb. If I were a wise man,

43

I'd do my part. What shall I give him? I'll give him my heart" (see stanza four of the hymn "In the Bleak Midwinter, words by Christinia G. Rosetti). In this resurrection challenge, we are asked to give God our hearts in Jesus. We believe the heart, mind, body, and soul shall be made to inherit the kingdom of God, imperishable and readied for all that the reign of God shall be. *(Vance P. Ross)*

---

# GIVE ME YOUR MONEY OR YOUR LIFE!

## INVOCATION

Dear Lord, we come this day to be reminded of what we too often forget, that you are doing new and wonderful things in our midst. But for some of us, the words of Jesus just rattle around in our minds and hearts like dry bones. Others of us are perplexed and skeptical; some of us are even angry with a Jesus who presumes to tell us how to live. We desire to hear the voice of God, but we are afraid of what we might have to give up.

In discomfort we listen as Jesus says that a person's "life does not consist in the abundance of possessions." Attune our ears to Jesus' words today and let them give us the wisdom that helps us understand this mystery that we call life. Amen.

## PRAYER OF CONFESSION

Benevolent God, Scripture tells us that every good and perfect gift comes from your generous hand. Why is it that we cannot bring ourselves to trust your munificence? We scurry here and there to try and secure our own lives and our own future. We worry ourselves sick plotting and conspiring ways to get ahead and keep in front of our rivals. We long to begin to trust again those blessed words of Jesus who taught your people, "Do not worry about tomorrow, for tomorrow will bring worries of its own. Today's trouble is enough for today" (Matthew 6:34). Yet, despite Jesus' magnificent promise, we frequently find ourselves of like mind with the psalmist who described us as we are: "It is in vain that you rise up early and go late to rest, eating the bread of anxious toil." May we come to trust the concluding affirmation that God "gives sleep to God's beloved" (Psalm 127:2).

Offer us comfort in your promise that every need we possess, Christ Jesus will gratify by his immeasurable riches and glory. It is for this freedom from anxiety that we pine. Give us this day the confidence in Christ that we may live in the liberation that only the gospel offers us. Indeed, may we be so bold as to live and trust in this gospel that we share it with all persons—everywhere. We pray this in the name of our Messiah. Amen.

# WORDS OF ASSURANCE: Philippians 4:19

God will fully satisfy every need of yours according to his riches in glory in Christ Jesus.

# PRAYER OF THANKSGIVING

As dawn broke this morning, O Gracious One, we saw your new creation beginning once again. We thank you that you deem it necessary and possible to share another day to proclaim your mighty works to our neighbors both far and near. We thank you that you give us the privilege of speaking the life-giving words of the gospel in love to our family, friends, and neighbors. O God, we thank you for the wonder gift of salvation that you offer to all people and for our part in your divine work. You made us worthy of such work through the life, death, and resurrection of Jesus, our Christ. Liberate us now to walk with you in newness of life. Amen.

# SCRIPTURE: Luke 12:13-21

# SERMON BRIEF: YOUR MONEY OR YOUR LIFE!

The old Jack Benny radio program had a sketch of Jack being robbed at gunpoint. Jack Benny was reported to be the tightest man alive when it came to money. In the sketch the robber says to Jack, "Hey bud, your money or your life." He got no reply. He said, "Hey, I said your money or your life." Jack replied, "Don't rush me. I'm thinking it over."

We laugh at that idea, but Jesus' parable makes us stop and think it over. The materialism of this era is well known. Many people live in order to accumulate more and more. But is it worthwhile? The parable of the rich fool makes us take a moment and reflect on the culture of consumerism.

## I. Possessions Can Own Us if We Aren't Careful

Why did the farmer think he had to use his large crop for himself? Selfishness becomes a habit. We do things without even considering other ways of thinking.

A story is told of a Russian czar who came upon a lonely sentry standing at attention in a secluded corner of the palace garden. "What are you guarding," asked the czar. "I don't know. The captain ordered me to this post," the sentry replied.

The czar called the captain. His answer: "Written regulations specify a guard was to be assigned to that area." The czar ordered a search to find out why.

The archives finally yielded the reason. Years before, Catherine the Great had planted a rose bush in that corner. She ordered a sentry to protect it for that one evening.

One hundred years later, sentries were still guarding the now barren spot.

Let's not let our possessions own us without even thinking about it.

## II. Sharing Our Possessions
## Is the Gospel Hope

Why did Jesus tell this parable? A man had asked him to tell his brother to divide the inheritance with him. Jesus did not respond directly. He simply asked who had appointed him as judge in such matters. Then he said, "Watch out! Be on your guard against all kinds of greed." Then he told the parable.

The possessive spirit of the farmer ruined him. It can ruin us, as well.

Back in 1998, ABC News presented a special program on greed with reporter John Stossel. The program began with a look at the Biltmore estate in North Carolina. Stossel pointed out the house is a gargantuan—two hundred fifty rooms. Yet it was all built for just one man to live in. The dining room is as high as a five-story building. The dining table seats sixty-four. The reporter said, "I guess when you're this rich, you make friends pretty easily. From here, you can take in the millions of dollars of art on the walls—Renoirs and Whistlers, Renaissance tapestries. Very beautiful, but isn't this greedy? Who needs a $100 million house?"

But a giving spirit can be our liberation. Take, for example, the well known story of a man who spoke with the Lord about heaven and hell. The Lord said to the man, "Come, I will show you hell." They entered a room where a group of people sat around a huge pot of stew. Everyone was famished—desperate and starving. Each held a spoon that reached the pot, but each spoon had a handle so much longer than each person's own arm that it could not be used to get the stew into each person's mouth. The suffering was terrible.

"Come, now I will show you heaven," the Lord said after a while. They entered another room, identical to the first—the pot of stew, the group of people, the same long-handled spoons. But there everyone was happy and well nourished.

"I don't understand," said the man. "Why are they happy here when they were miserable in the other room and everything was the same?"

The Lord smiled, "Ah, it is simple," he said. "Here they have learned to feed each other."

The old question is still real: your money or your life? Which do you choose? (*Don M. Aycock*)

## BENEDICTION

O God, as you send us into your world, make us a generous people sharing your love and mercy, in the name of the creator, the redeemer, and the sustainer. Amen.

# CHAPTER TWELVE

# HOLD NOTHING BACK

## CALL TO WORSHIP: Psalm 65:1-2, 9-13

Praise is due to you,
  O God, in Zion;
and to you shall vows be performed,
  **O you who answer prayer!**
**To you all flesh shall come.**
You visit the earth and water it,
  you greatly enrich it;
the river of God is full of water;
  you provide the people with grain,
  for so you have prepared it.
**You water its furrows abundantly,**
  **settling its ridges,**
**softening it with showers,**
  **and blessing its growth.**
You crown the year with your bounty;
  your wagon tracks overflow with richness.
**The pastures of the wilderness overflow,**
  **the hills gird themselves with joy,**
*All:* **the meadows clothe themselves with flocks,**
      **the valleys deck themselves with grain,**
      **they shout and sing together for joy.**

# Prayer of Confession

O Lord, holy and righteous God, hear the prayer of our hearts. We reflect upon our sin before you and before our sisters and brothers. The depths of your love for us, convicts us of our sin and we are cut to the quick. We throw ourselves upon your boundless mercy and ask you for forgiveness. Just as you have run the good race before us, set us on the path that leads to you and help us repent of our sin as we turn toward you. In Jesus we recognize the perfect model for faithfulness, and yet we have failed to follow the Christ. Teach us to recognize that when we gaze upon Jesus, we see as much of you, O God, as we can ever see on this side of death. Grant to us a new beginning and a fresh start so that we might, once again, be inspired to follow the Risen Christ and run our race boldly in faith. Make us bold in our living, bold in our confidence, and bold in our proclamation of our Lord. Let us hold nothing back. In the name of Jesus, we pray. Amen.

# Words of Assurance

In the name of Jesus Christ, God Almighty offers you new life in Christ. Take this inexpressible gift and live fully and rightly in the world God has given us as a precious gift. Our gift back to God is to care for our world as disciples of Jesus. Amen.

# Prayer before the Reading of Holy Scripture

Author of life everlasting, teach us through the holy word we are about to hear. May it inspire in us a deep desire for godly living and remind us that you poured out your life for us and for the salvation of the world. In Jesus' name we pray. Amen.

# SCRIPTURE: 2 Timothy 4:6-8, 16-18

# SERMON BRIEF: HOLD NOTHING BACK

The author of 2 Timothy closes the letter with a toast—his life is poured out like a libation. Cheers! Here's looking at you!

But libation, taken seriously, also means a life poured out in the form of costly sacrifice—like wine spilled on the altar. This text is analogous with Romans 12 where Paul admonishes the faithful to present their very "bodies as a living sacrifice" to God (12:1). Hold nothing back.

The writer tells of his struggles: "I have fought the good fight, I have finished the race, I have kept the faith." The crown awaits the writer. Is this some kind of holy boasting, self-righteous crowing? I think not. Here is a desperate man who will use every occasion, even the risk of arrogance, as a means to preach the salvation story and to encourage the fainthearted.

Many of his disciples have left him. The writer uses the language and metaphor of the Olympic games to give Timothy a pep talk. Timothy knows about the long distance runner who, if he is to win, must find the strength that he doesn't have. The runner must save up for that last kick needed to push beyond his or her endurance, and at the breathless point of needing oxygen, will finally feel the snap of the finish line string. In that moment of ecstasy he knows that the race is run, the fight is finished, and the faith is secure.

Poet Donald Hall, in telling of his struggle to write a good poem, tells would-be poets to hold nothing back. Put everything out that can possibly belong in that poem or story. Don't save anything for the next one. That's the only way to work. That is the only way to live (Bill D. Moyers, *Language of Life: A Festival of Poets* [New York: Doubleday, 1995], 157).

A saying, sometimes attributed to Voltaire, puts it even better, "The best is the enemy of the good." In a world that will put up with "that's pretty good," 2 Timothy challenges us to do our best, to pay up personally even to the point of pouring out our lives as living sacrifice.

A friend tells of a young man who canceled his cable television subscription because he wished to make a sacrificial gift to his church each month. The cable company called to discover why he canceled service. The young man explained that he did it so he could make a sacrificial gift. "Sir, said the representative, can you give me another reason? We don't have a category for sacrifice on our cancel list." So it goes.

The writer of 2 Timothy ends the letter with one true boast— to God be the glory. He means the God who made the sacrifice that is demanded and proved in the death and resurrection of Jesus, that the faithful will be delivered from every evil attack and kept safe. Glory to God forever. Amen. *(William Cotton)*

---

# CHAPTER THIRTEEN

# WHO DO YOU REALLY WANT TO BE?

## PRAYER FOR THE BEGINNING OF WORSHIP

O God, the psalmist had it right when he sang: "I will both lie down and sleep in peace; for you alone, O LORD, make me lie down in safety" (Psalm 4:8). As we worship this morning, remind us that you bless us beyond our most untamed dreams. You plant within our hearts the revelation of the world, as it ought to be. You give us glimpses of your kingdom, visions of your glory, participation in your mission and ministry. Help us plant the seeds of your kingdom everywhere we go whether it is our school, our grocery, our restaurant, our park, our factory, or our living room. Inspire us this day by your Holy Spirit so that we may live into the fullness of life for which you created all of us. Amen.

## PASTORAL PRAYER

Lord of heaven and earth, we worship you this day in praise and thanksgiving. We praise you for you place us in a wonderful world that is your creation and your creation alone. You placed us in this glorious garden and gave it to us as our earthly home. All that you asked of us is that we cultivate it and keep it as a holy trust. We thank you that you charged us with your creation. Yet we turn away from you, seeking our own glory with lust and greed. We want to be good stewards, but we are torn; sometimes we feel that you gave us a raw deal. Our world is filled with sorrow and suffering and we wonder where you are. Would that you might walk in our garden in the breezy time of day so that we could ask you some hard questions. Yet you did come to walk with us in the person of your son, Jesus. But that was long ago and far away. Where are you now—so where are you now? You are with us, leading us in the paths of righteousness, quenching our thirst in still waters, restoring our souls for your name's sake even when we walk through the valley of the shadow of death. You are with me. You are with us. Open our eyes. Open our hearts for our re-creation. Inspire in us a care for your earth, even as you care for us.

Help us see that we are workers in your vineyard and inspire in us a desire to share its bounty with those in need. Place in our minds and hearts a craving to share the vineyard's yield with those who are in need—orphans, widows, and those who sojourn among us. Let us call every person a sister or brother of sacred worth. And more than anything, O God, help us learn to dwell in peace, your shalom. In Jesus' name we pray. Amen.

## SCRIPTURE: Matthew 21:33-46

## SERMON BRIEF: OWNERS OR SHARECROPPERS?

It's October, the time of harvest. And, it's the first Sunday of October, the time when many Christians observe World Communion Sunday. Few scriptures could be more appropriate for this day than this parable of harvest. It is set in a vineyard, a common image for the kingdom of God. It concerns the state of affairs in the commonwealth of God. On this day, diverse groups within God's family lean forward to hear a story of peculiar relevance from Jesus.

Jesus works with material that's familiar to his listeners. He uses words and images from Isaiah's "Song of the Unfruitful Vineyard" (Isaiah 5:1-7). As in Isaiah, a landowner painstakingly establishes a vineyard. The vineyard in Isaiah yields wild grapes rather than grapes. The vineyard here produces an adequate crop, but the tenants refuse to turn over produce to the owner. Both stories present injustices that cry for remedy.

The parable's landowner affords us a glimpse of the character of God, while the tenants resemble us. God has created a wonderful world in which each of us has a place, and an opportunity for prosperity. God has attended to every detail of the creation. In this vineyard we have every reason to rejoice in the blessings that the Creator has bestowed on us and to share the riches with others and with God. No other arrangement seems fair.

Unfortunately, our story, like the story here, packs a rude surprise. We present-day tenants want to keep all of the produce for ourselves! In fact, we, too, want to be installed as owners. We justify it in our thoughts: "We have tilled the soil, tended to the crop, kept watch over it night and day. Without us there would be no crop! Why should the owner get any of the crop, let alone the lion's share of it?"

We, like the original tenants, contemplate the distance between the owner and ourselves. We reason, "Why should we pay him? He's too far away to touch us directly. He may never come back! He has many other vineyards, and we need the produce more than he does."

The tenants in the parable are traditionally called "wicked" more for their violence than their greed. In Matthew 11:12 Jesus has already said, "From the days of John the Baptist until now the kingdom of heaven has suffered violence, and the violent take it by force." From the time of Cain and Abel we humans have shown an astonishing capacity for violence. We let no one, not even God, stand in our way.

The most amazing feature of the parable is the forbearance of the landowner. He ends up with no rent, no honor, no servants, no son, and no vineyard! This is an odd depiction of our Creator God, who has a strange vulnerability to us creatures. God comes to us in such ways that we can almost always turn God down. Frederick Buechner observes that "God puts himself at our mercy not only in the sense of the suffering that we can cause him by our blindness and coldness and cruelty, but the suffering that we can cause him simply by suffering ourselves." When someone we love suffers, we suffer with him because the suffering and the love are one (*The Hungering Dark* [San Francisco: Harper, 1985], 14). Because of God's unsurpassable love for us there seem to be no limits to the self-humiliation to which the divine will descend in pursuit of us. That's love's nature.

Jesus' story says that in God's commonwealth all of us are sharecroppers, not owners. We tend the earth and its riches on the Creator's behalf. Though we have delusions of ownership, we are here only through the generosity of the Owner, who seeks tenants who will share the harvest generously.

The issue of sharing is crucial. How much of the produce are we using to build a commonwealth of justice and love, and how much are we using to feed our own worldly status? Only generous people can reflect God's image in a broken world. If we aim to be good neighbors and faithful stewards on this World Communion Sunday, we must work to put the entire crop into God's hands. The One who created it and made it grow is also the One most able to distribute the bounty for the blessing of all. (*Sandy Wylie*)

## BENEDICTION

Now may the God of peace, who brought our Lord Jesus back from the dead, heal our own spiritual deadness. May the Good Shepherd, by the blood of the eternal covenant, make you complete in every good thing so that you may do God's will to live faith, shout hope, and love one another. Amen.

# CHAPTER FOURTEEN

# PUTTING YOUR MONEY WHERE YOUR MOUTH IS

## INVOCATION

Grant us in this hour of worship, O Lord, a glimpse of your majesty and power. Let us join our hands, voices, and hearts in magnifying your holy name. As we pray, send your spirit upon us so that we might experience your promised salvation given to us through the word of Scripture. Let that word be our strength and shield. Let us now join our sisters and brothers around the world and through the centuries to call upon the name of Jesus Christ, our Lord and Savior. It is in Christ's name that we pray. Amen.

## PRAYER OF CONFESSION

To you we lift up our hearts, O Lord our God. As we reflect upon our lives as your children, we recognize that we have fallen short. We want to be faithful disciples, but we let impediments stand in our path. We let a world that seldom honors you and refuses to recognize your mighty hand dictate our relationship to you. We fail to understand the nature of servanthood. We fail to be an obedient church. We let petty jealousies and rivalries interfere with our ministries. We confess that we are constantly tempted to become our own masters. Yet you have told us that the greatest among us will be a servant of all. We act as if we don't believe you.

Provide us a vision of your realm so that we can again see the power of your purpose for us and for your world. Help us lift our gaze from our personal troubles and needs, so that we can see the suffering and desperation of others. Remind us once again that love is stronger than hate, and that hope overcomes despair— even when this is so difficult for us to discern. Let us stand on the promise that nothing can separate us from the love of God in Christ Jesus. Now equip and empower us for God's gracious work in our church, in our community, and in our world. Renew our spirits; refresh our souls; give us clean hearts. We humbly pray this in Jesus' name. Amen.

## WORDS OF ASSURANCE: John 3:16

For God so loved the world that he gave his only Son, so that everyone who believes in him may not perish but may have eternal life.

## SCRIPTURE: 2 Corinthians 8:1-15

## SERMON BRIEF: GRACIOUS GIVING

Paul opens this passage by sharing news of the grace of the Macedonian churches. While struggling themselves, "their abundant joy and their extreme poverty have overflowed in a wealth of generosity on their part" (8:2). He also shares that they gave voluntarily and lays out two principles for spiritual stewardship and generosity. First, "they gave themselves first to the Lord" (8:5). Second, they gave of themselves to others. These principles form the crucial backdrop for the passage that begins in verse 7 with the plea that the Corinthians themselves should excel in "this generous undertaking."

Although verse 8 opens with the acknowledgment that the offering for others is not a command, Paul nonetheless states it in the strongest language. He says it is a "testing." Verse 9 heightens this sense of expectancy when Paul moves to exhortation, using the grace of the Lord as a model for the Corinthian church. In almost blunt terms, the self-offering of Christ is to become a model for our financial offering toward others. In verse 10, Paul again states that, while this is only his opinion, he feels strongly that this work, so nobly begun, must now be completed.

Verse 11 introduces a new theme. Here, Paul explicitly states that one should give in accordance with his or her means. With verse 12, he returns us again to the theme that joyful, willful giving reflects one's commitment to Christ and a commitment to God's people. In a larger sense, this section of the passage invites us to match our deeds to our words. In the more colloquial phrase, we might say, "Put your money where your mouth is." Paul does so in the context of understanding that gracious giving is evaluated, not on the basis of the amount given, but rather on the connection between the spirit of giving and the resources one has to offer. Verse 15 drives this point home. "The one who had much did not have too much, and the one who had little did not have too little." Because the Corinthians have an abundance to share, they are expected, as a faithful people, to help their brothers and sisters in Jerusalem. It should be noted further that verse 15 is a quotation from Exodus 16:18.

Taken as a whole, Paul makes a strong, though not commanding, plea for the voluntary, joyful support of the needs of the poor beyond the local community of faith. The Christian's duty is not merely to one's own circle of friends or church community. Christian duty reaches to the wider world. The Gentile Christians of Corinth are called to help the Jewish Christians of Jerusalem because of the abundance of God's gifts and, in so doing, are to use Christ as the model, giving according to their means in faithfulness to the work of the Lord.

Choices for freedom in ordinary lives are frequently, perhaps constantly, connected to money. The instruction of the Lord to those of us who live in the abundance of Western civilization is gripping. Our abundance is to be used to meet the needs of others. The gifts God has given us are not to control us, but to graciously be used as the Lord graciously gave of himself in the love and care of the poor and the needy. (*Mike Lowry*)

# CHAPTER FIFTEEN

# GOD, YOU'VE GOT TO BE KIDDING

## CALL TO WORSHIP: Psalm 103:1-5, 22

Bless the LORD, O my soul,
  and all that is within me,
  bless his holy name.
**Bless the LORD, O my soul,**
  **and do not forget all his benefits—**
**who forgives all your iniquity,**
  **who heals all your diseases.**
Who redeems your life from the Pit,
  who crowns you with steadfast love and mercy,
who satisfies you with good as long as you live
  so that your youth is renewed like the eagle's.
**Bless the LORD, all his works,**
  **in all places of his dominion.**
*All:* **Bless the LORD, O my soul.**

## OFFERTORY PRAYER

O God, you teach in the Holy Scriptures that we are to care for those who have little and are poor. Remind us that as we give our offering that we are contributing to those who are the least, the lost, and the last. Daily may we remember the words of Jesus, who taught us, "Truly I tell you, just as you did it to one of the least of these who are members of my family, you did it to me" (Matthew 25:40). Help us remember just how much we truly have. Now, consecrate these gifts in the name of Jesus the Christ and our Messiah. Amen.

# PASTORAL PRAYER

O Lord of All, hear our prayers today as we pour out our spirits like oil upon your holy altar. Make our prayers leap to life as we acknowledge you as the sovereign of the universe. You have spoken to us through the law and prophets. You have spoken to us through the Hebrew hymns we call the Psalms. You have communicated an understanding of yourself through the writings of our own New Testament. But most decisively, you give us your most direct self-communication through the gospel of Jesus Christ, even here, even now. It is you in whom we move and live and have our being.

Let us once again take heart in your lessons of life. May we see in the teachings, the life, the death, and the resurrection of Christ a better way of living life abundantly. You incarnated the wisdom of the ages in the life of your son, Jesus. Through Jesus you show us right living and right relationship to you and to each other. Through your church you give us the possibility to incarnate your plans in the world. Heal us of our divisions. Heal us of our strife. We know we are richly blessed. Let us use our blessings to bless others.

Lord, we know we have much and that much is expected of us. We feel guilty and ashamed when we think of how little we share with others. And perhaps we need to. Use our guilt and shame to motivate us to live righteously. Protect us from living self-righteously, sitting in judgment of others. Keep our guilt and shame from paralyzing us or trying to find others to blame. Help us learn from our limitations and failures. Give us the courage to reflect your image in the world, not for our glory, but for yours. Free us for joyful obedience; give us a way out of no way. And always Lord, let Jesus' prayer, "not my will but yours be done," be our prayer. We pray this and all things in Jesus' holy name. Amen.

## SCRIPTURE: Mark 10:17-31

## SERMON BRIEF: TO WHOM MUCH IS GIVEN

The story of the rich man trying to inherit eternal life is traditionally used to admonish the wealthy. It is natural to paint an ugly picture of this man. One can imagine him in brightly colored robes, perhaps with gilded accents; he is clean-shaven with a good composure. He speaks eloquently and probably commands respect when he is in a crowd. He has most likely had an easy life with an exotic and lavish upbringing. It is easy not to like him. It is easy to think of him as having hoarded his wealth, not giving to the poor or to his church. He may be getting to the end of his life and wants to ensure his eternity. Surely, we would like to think, that is why he approaches Jesus.

Take a closer look at this passage and Jesus' words and actions toward the rich man reveal a different story. As the man approaches Jesus, he calls him "Good Teacher." He knows who Jesus is and what his ministry is about. When Jesus addresses him he says, "You know the commandments," identifying that he is a knowledgeable man. After the man claims to have kept all the commandments, the text reveals, "Jesus . . . loved him and said, 'You lack one thing.'" Jesus does not condemn him or belittle him for the way he has handled his wealth. Rather, Jesus loves the man and affirms him for following the commandments but does mention that the man lacks one thing. Instead of focusing on what he has not done, Jesus loves him for the commandments he has honored.

When hearing that he must sell his possessions and give the money to the poor before he follows Jesus, the rich man is shocked and leaves in a grievous state. This prompts a harsh statement from Jesus as he exclaims that it will be difficult for the rich to enter the kingdom of God. This proclamation perplexes the disciples, perhaps because it does not apply to them. Thus Jesus makes his exclamation more personal. "Children, how hard it is to enter the kingdom of God!" (v. 24). This statement applies to everyone; this exclamation means everyone, including the disciples, will have a difficult time entering the kingdom of God. Jesus' focus is no longer on the rich man trying to enter the kingdom of God; rather Jesus explains that everyone needs God's help when trying to accomplish, as Jesus calls it, the impossible.

This passage concludes with a distorted version of what has come to be a key phrase of the Christian faith. We typically quote, "So the last will be first, and the first will be last," as it is written in the Gospel of Matthew (20:16). But Mark 10:31 reads: "But many who are first will be last, and the last will be first." There is great importance in Jesus using the word *many* in this verse. Since Jesus does not say that all who are first will be last—only "many" of them—perhaps there is hope for the rich man of this story.

Too often we would like to think that those who are ranked first in this life—those who are wealthy and seem to have easy lives—will have their time of hardship in the future. They will be last in line for the kingdom of God, behind people like some of us who have dedicated our time and energy to the perpetuation of Jesus' ministry. Jesus' final statement in this story helps us to not be so judgmental. Because Jesus loved and affirmed the rich man, he gives him hope in the kingdom of God. Perhaps we should also follow Jesus' example. Jesus loves and affirms those who do their best to obey the commandments and who may come up short. We follow Jesus' example, lest we also find ourselves last. (*Victoria Atkinson White*)

---

# CHAPTER SIXTEEN

# BUT IT'S NOT WHAT I SIGNED UP FOR!

## PRAYER TO BEGIN WORSHIP

As we worship and begin our Sabbath rest, O Lord of the Sabbath, renew and refresh our spirits. When we worship we remember your mighty acts of old. We remember how you brought the Hebrews out of the land of bondage "by a mighty hand and an outstretched arm," and that you continually rescue your people. We also remember how you brought your people to a land flowing with milk and honey. All these are gifts we, too, may claim. Most especially we pray that we might hear the stories of Jesus who came to save us from our sin and give us abundant life. As we worship, wake us up to your glory that surrounds us in this place. Energize us with the fresh air of your Holy Spirit. In the name of Jesus, we pray. Amen.

## PRAYER OF CONFESSION

Lord, we have tried to be your obedient children, but life in the world is tough. It sometimes seems that the harder we work, the less we see for our efforts. We confess that many of us are afraid to talk to people about Jesus. We are afraid of what others might think of us; we are afraid of failing; we are afraid of looking foolish. Others of us prefer to spin the truth rather than speak the truth. Some of us are hurting. Some are angry. Some are defeated. We have all fallen short of your glory. We want you to give us all that we desire, but often we only want to give you a little in return. Even so we all need your grace to light the darkness in our lives. We need your joy, peace, patience, gentleness, kindness, self-control, goodness that can only come from abiding daily in your Word. We know that if we put our efforts into living graciously with you, we will reap benefit. Help us continually turn toward you. We confess this day that we cannot do your work or ours by ourselves. We need more—we need you.

We confess that we need to trust you and have faith that your way of loving grace is the way to people's hearts. Therefore, we pray, O God, that you help us stop simply talking about love—and simply be more loving. We pray, O God, that you inspire us to stop merely speaking about justice—and simply be more just. Where we are weak, make us strong. We may be defeated but with you, O God, we will never be destroyed. Where our faith lags, make your grace run ahead to meet us at our points of need. We pray this in the name of the one who offers us eternal life. Amen.

## WORDS OF ASSURANCE: Matthew 7:7-8

Ask, and it will be given you; search, and you will find; knock, and the door will be opened for you. For everyone who asks receives, and everyone who searches finds, and for everyone who knocks, the door will be opened.

## SCRIPTURE: Luke 14:25-33

## SERMON BRIEF: IT'S ALL OR NOTHING

Recently our daughter came home from school and asked if I would bake a cake for a dinner theater her drama class was sponsoring. I readily agreed. I didn't realize, until she came home later in the week with bags of ingredients, that we had signed up to make all the cakes for two hundred people. That wasn't quite what I thought I was signing up for!

You may have had similar experiences, Did you agree to sit on a committee that someone told you would take a minimal investment, only to find it all consuming? Did you sign up for the video or CD club without reading the fine print that contained the details of how much it would cost to fulfill your obligation? In today's passage, Jesus is seeking to avoid any such misunderstandings. Jesus wants to be sure that folks know just what the cost of following him will be.

As the story opens, the scene has shifted from the intimate mealtimes at the beginning of the chapter. Jesus is back on the road to Jerusalem, and large crowds are traveling with him. Wisely, Jesus is not overly impressed by the size of the crowd. He rightly suspects that they are along for the ride, that they are even more unsuspecting than the disciples about what lies ahead. Cutting right to the chase, Jesus turns and makes it clear just what is expected of those who truly wish to follow.

Without historical context, Jesus' first words seem harsh and totally out of character. How can the Jesus who has preached radical love and inclusion suddenly call for his followers to hate father and mother, wife and children, brothers and sisters? To understand his intent, we must set aside the emotions of anger and hostility that we associate with the word *hate*. Here, *hate* is a Semitic expression of exaggeration used to mean "turn away from" or "separate from." Jesus is saying that not only is the call to discipleship the highest calling but it also reorders and redefines every other relationship we are a part of. "Count the cost," Jesus says.

Next, Jesus warns the crowd that they must carry their cross and follow him. In our society, our "cross to bear" is often seen as a problem or circumstance that we have no control over, something that we had no choice in assuming. Jesus' intent here is different. We are called to make a willing and intentional choice to take up our crosses and follow.

Jesus illustrates his point with two parables. In the first, a farmer is considering building an observation tower in his field. In the second, a king is discerning whether he has adequate resources to wage war on his enemy. The point is clear. All people, rural and urban, rich and poor have the same choice to make. The time of decision has come. Do we have what it takes to see the project through to the end? Jesus calls us to consider our answers carefully and not to respond without careful consideration. For us, much more is at stake than embarrassment in front of the neighbors or defeat at the hands of an enemy.

Although we must all make the same decision about whether or not we are willing to pay the price to follow, it may cost us different things. For some it may cost us the reordering of relationships, for others the price may be giving up possessions. For still others, the investment may be in the form of time or energy. Whatever the price, it will be costly. The journey to Jerusalem cost God and Jesus everything. How can we expect to pay less? (*Tracy Hartman*)

## BENEDICTION

May you go into the world as a transformed child of God and take with you the wisdom that God alone offers. Jesus himself told us that we are the salt of the earth and we are the light of the world. Go, salt and light the world in the name of the Father, the Son, and the Holy Spirit. Amen.

# CHAPTER SEVENTEEN

# GIVE ME MORE THAN POSSESSIONS

## PRAYER FOR THE CHURCH

Gracious God, our assembly today is part of what Paul called "the body of Christ." This is an awesome gift and privilege for us. We know that we cannot live up to the promises that you, through the church, hold out for the world—but we are willing to try. Lord, we are able. Therefore, Gracious God, send your Holy Spirit upon us and make us strong in faith, firm in hope, steadfast in love. Give us vision and discernment to do your will here on earth and, if it may please you, ratify the works of our hands. Our message is: Christ has died; Christ has risen; Christ will come again. Help us stay on message bringing truth and justice in the way of Christ. Remind us that forgiveness is one of our strong spiritual weapons and please, O Lord, remove our sinful pride. Yet, fill us with the confidence befitting your children. Amen.

## OFFERTORY PRAYER

Dear Lord, as we dedicate these gifts at your altar remind us of Paul's words when he wrote to the church at Galatia: "So then, whenever we have an opportunity, let us work for the good of all, and especially for those of the family of faith" (Galatians 6:10). Amen.

# PRAYER BEFORE THE READING OF HOLY SCRIPTURE

O Author of Life, who ordered our Bible, work your grace and the miracle of faith once again through the reading of these sacred texts. You, O God, inspired those who passed scripture's wise tradition on to us as a sacred covenant. May our scripture be for us a portal into life abundant. We pray this in Jesus' name. Amen.

## SCRIPTURE: Luke 16:19-31

# SERMON BRIEF: MORE THAN POSSESSIONS

Luke seeks in this passage to continue his concern around the place of stewardship in the life of a follower of Christ. The key to understanding this passage is discovered in verse 31 as Abraham responds to the rich man by saying, "If they do not listen to Moses and the prophets, neither will they be convinced even if someone rises from the dead." The response frames all that precedes it in the parable. The inference here is that evidently the rich man has come to the realization that the reason for his suffering is linked to his lack of interpretation of the law and the prophets, or his misinterpretation of them. One can feel his sense of failure as he begs Abraham to use different means to warn his family and friends who are still living so that they will not make the same mistake he has. The theme of this story is that there are consequences to what we do with what God gives us, especially as it relates to following the guidance God has offered through Scripture.

This is not a popular story to preach in the church of a culture like ours. Prosperity theology runs amok in the church today as we attempt to not only justify our wealth, but also to go so far as to say that it is a sign of how God has blessed us. Jesus told this parable as a response to such thinking in the lives of the Pharisees. Using the Deuteronomic law as a foundation of their attitudes surrounding their wealth, they sought to tie that wealth to their faith as a sign of God blessing them for being righteous in the eyes of God.

Jesus turns such thinking on its ear. Jesus seeks to reinterpret the law and the prophets for his hearers as he places the responsibility for wealth and what one does with it squarely on their shoulders. Once again we find the theme of stewardship and its prominent place in the kingdom. The rich man suffers in the afterlife because of his inattention to being responsible with his great wealth during his earthly fife, especially as it related to the poor. Jesus proclaims that in the kingdom of God people must respond to all that God has given them in a way that is fair and responsible, and with much love and compassion.

Jesus also seeks in this passage to relate that God holds us all accountable for our own life, for all that we are, and for all that we own. Both Lazarus and the rich man are held responsible for who they were and what they did—or did not do—with what they had. The rich man's pleading for someone to warn his brothers goes unheeded as Jesus plainly states that God has given everyone the same guides to life. Our lives will be judged according to our response to those guides and their instructions. Such teaching will not be popular in a culture obsessed with instant gratification, the pursuit of wealth, and the "right" to fifteen minutes of fame. And yet, the church must boldly proclaim this countercultural message, which demands accountability in relation to one's possessions. Such accountability also includes our interpretation of the Scripture that God has entrusted to us and how that interpretation plays out in our lives.

In 1962, four young musicians auditioned for Decca Records. The record executives dismissed them saying, "We don't like their sound. Groups of guitars are on the way out." As a result, the Beatles left without a contract. We had best be careful about what we base our decisions on in life. Jesus' parable reminds us of the implications and consequences of such decision-making. After all, life, according to this parable, is about much more than possessions. (*Travis Franklin*)

## BENEDICTION: 2 Corinthians 13:13

Now go with the knowledge that your salvation is a consequence of God's steadfast lovingkindness through Christ Jesus. The grace of the Lord Jesus Christ, the love of God, and the communion of the Holy Spirit be with all of you.

# CHAPTER EIGHTEEN

# YES, SOMETIMES THE DIRECTIONS DO HELP

## INVOCATION

God of Glory, send your spirit upon us gathered in this sanctuary as we worship and magnify your holy name. Remind us once again that the gate that leads to you is, in Jesus' words, "narrow and the road is hard that leads to life." Yet, inspire us despite the difficulties of discipleship to recognize that our following of Jesus is that which leads to eternal life—life that we call abundant. Divest us of our false assumptions that lead to unwise decisions. Help us make that life-saving decision to follow Jesus; not only with our lips, but also with the actions that following Jesus calls forth from us. Make us people who see that in giving life we receive it and make it so among us today. In Jesus' name we pray. Amen.

## PRAYER BEFORE THE READING OF HOLY SCRIPTURE

As we gather before our sacred Scripture, O God, make our ears attentive to the words you offer us through the Bible's prophets, seers, historians, and composers. Let us marinate our spirits within the blessed accounts of people like us who struggle between grace and sin, love and hate, blessings and curses. Help us choose, like Mary, the better portion; and may your Holy Word inspire us to, once again, be your faithful people. Amen.

## SCRIPTURE: Mark 10:17-31

## SERMON BRIEF: WHEN YOU LACK JUST ONE THING

A few years ago I was putting together a white, laminated bookshelf for my daughter. The piece of furniture was simple, so I tossed the directions aside. After placing all the pieces on the floor exactly as they should be assembled, I proceeded to attach the horizontal boards to one of the vertical boards, using the supplied bag of wooden dowels, screws, and locking inserts. As soon as I finished one side, I immediately started on the other side. Starting at the top of the bookshelf, one by one I locked the shelves into place. Only the bottom shelf remained. I reached into the plastic bag to grab the last screw, but the bag was empty. Thinking the screw must have fallen out of the bag, I searched the box that the pieces came in as well as the room. The only thing that I found was the direction that I had laid aside earlier.

I glanced at the directions, hoping to discover that somehow I had made a mistake and put a screw where it didn't belong. The very first statement on the directions was in bold print and surrounded by a border: "Before you begin, please read the entire instructions and make sure you have all the necessary parts and tools required."

Determined to make it work, I tried improvising. Every time I failed I became angrier and angrier. When I finally called the store and informed them of the problem, the manager said he was sorry and that he would be happy to give me another bookshelf, if I returned the other. I protested, "You mean, I have to disassemble this bookshelf and return it for an unassembled bookshelf just because one screw is missing?"

Sometimes, lacking just one thing can be terribly frustrating.

Of all the people who ever came to Jesus, the rich young ruler is one of the few who was sent away worse off than when he arrived. Yet he had so much in his favor. He was a young man with tremendous potential (see Matthew 19:22). He was respected by others and held some ruling office (Luke 18:18). He had high morals and a sincere desire for spiritual things. In many ways, he was an ideal young man and a high achiever.

Kneeling before Jesus, the young man asked, "Good Teacher, what must I do to inherit eternal life?" His question was right, but his assumptions were wrong. His question was based on at least three false assumptions. His first assumption was that *goodness could be achieved.* His second assumption was that *eternal life could be earned.* His third assumption was that *everything could be bought for a price, including eternal life.*

Jesus shattered all three assumptions. Jesus reminded him that "no one is good but God" (v. 18). While the young man was faithful in some things (vv. 19-20), he still lacked one thing. Jesus identified the one thing that stood between the rich young ruler and God when he said, "Go, sell what you own, and give the money to the poor." That was more than the young man was willing to do. The rich young man was so close, but yet so far away. He "went away grieving, for he had many possessions" (v. 22).

Jesus shatters the last false assumption by reminding the disciples that the kingdom of God is not for sale. The kingdom of God does not come as a result of our own effort and achievements; it is the result of God's initiative and grace. When the disciples asked, "[If the rich man can't be saved], then who can be saved?" (v. 26), Jesus answered, "For mortals it is impossible, but not for God; for God all things are possible" (v. 27).

Barbara Brown Taylor captures the essence of the encounter: "[It] is not a story about money, because, if it were, we could buy our way into heaven by cashing in our chips right now, and you know that is not so. None of us earns eternal life, no matter what we do. We can keep the Commandments until we are blue in the face; we can sign our paychecks over to Mother Teresa and rattle tin cups for our supper without ever earning a place at the banquet table of God. The kingdom of God is not for sale. It never has been; it never will be. The poor cannot buy it with their poverty, and the rich cannot buy it with their riches. The kingdom of God is a consummate gift" (*The Preaching Life* [Boston: Cowley Publications, 1993], 122).

Grace, the unmerited favor of God, is the one thing that you and I cannot lack if we wish to enter the kingdom of God. (*Bob Buchanan*)

# BENEDICTION

Friends, our Scripture tells us that "for God all things are possible." Therefore, whatever you face in life, remember that God walks before you, with you, and behind you. God is in all, over all, and under all; thus, take heart and believe in God's mighty promises in Jesus Christ. Go and claim this divine promise for your mortal life! Amen.

# CHAPTER NINETEEN

# GETTING WHAT WE PAY FOR... OR NOT

## CALL TO WORSHIP: Psalm 13

How long, O LORD? Will you forget me forever?
How long will you hide your face from me?
**How long must I bear pain in my soul,**
**and have sorrow in my heart all day long?**
**How long shall my enemy be exalted over me?**
Consider and answer me, O LORD my God!
Give light to my eyes, or I will sleep the sleep of death,
and my enemy will say, "I have prevailed";
my foes will rejoice because I am shaken.
*All:* **But I trusted in your steadfast love;**
**my heart shall rejoice in your salvation.**
**I will sing to the LORD,**
**because he has dealt bountifully with me.**

## PASTORAL PRAYER

We are your people, Gracious Lord, because we think that we love you above all else. Yet, in our most honest moments, we must confess that there are many things in our lives, in our thoughts, and in our actions, that an unbiased observer would find curious because we offer contrary evidence. We put other gods before you—success, money, fame, power, even life itself. We are well intentioned. We do not mean to be faithless, but the pressures of job, school, family, and our need for acceptance seduce us to be less than who you call us to be. Sometimes we worship little gods instead of you, Almighty God. Forgive us and offer us new glimpses into the heavenly realms so that we might once again catch a vision of the divine truth that you offer to us. Surround us again with your comforting spirit and calm our anxious lives. Remind us that sin lurks; and only by staying close to you, through the means of grace, can we dodge the temptations that seek our very lives. Remind us that freedom, true freedom, is a gracious gift. Let us be your instruments of righteousness in this world. Let the world see in us your gifts of peace, patience, kindness, gentleness, goodness, and self-control. Your grace is sufficient we know. Now help us trust and believe in your steadfast lovingkindness with all our heart, mind, and strength as we freely serve our neighbors as ourselves. We pray in the name of Jesus, the "faithful witness, the firstborn of the dead, and the ruler of the kings of the earth" (Revelation 1:5).

## OFFERTORY PRAYER

As your people, Lord, we want to do the right and righteous thing for the sake of Jesus' kingdom, but we are anxious and afraid. We pray "give us this day our daily bread," but we worry what if . . .

Give us the courage and confidence to give of our time and treasure in a way that reveals authentic confidence in your promise to always abide with us. Make us a generous people who are freed from worry and anxiety about the things of the earth. Bless these gifts we offer you as a reflection of our true faith. Amen.

# SCRIPTURE: Romans 6:12-23

# SERMON BRIEF: CHOOSING OUR PAY

The old adage says, "We get what we pay for." If we buy a cheap TV, we ought not to be surprised if it goes on the blink in a few months, or the picture is not as sharp as the one on the expensive set. If we want quality, we have to pay for it.

In a similar sense, what we get out of life depends on what we put into it. If we seek after cheap values and evil ends, we should not be surprised when life pays us back with emptiness, guilt, and meaninglessness. If we want the most out of life, we need to give ourselves to the highest and best values we can—the values seen in Christ.

This is the message Paul gives in these words of Scripture. There seem to be three movements.

## I. Soldiers—Giving the Best (vv. 12-14)

Paul talked about yielding their "members" to God. This referred to a soldier's weapons, weapons offered in service. A soldier would hold nothing back in his commitment to a cause. If his life were demanded, it would be given. That was the commitment of a soldier.

Like a soldier, the disciples of Christ should yield everything to the cause. The weapons of their lives—hands, feet, eyes, minds, hearts, lives—all needed to be committed to serving Christ. There were plenty of people committed to serving evil in the world. Paul stated that, before Christ came to them, that was what they were doing, being instruments of wickedness. That changed. Now they were instruments of righteousness. The commitment given to evil was now transferred to Christ.

Christ held nothing back from us. We are to hold nothing back from Christ. Whatever it takes to serve, will we give it?

## II. Slavery—To What or to Whom? (vv. 15-19)

What does it mean to be free? Strangely, the answer to that question is seen in the imagery that Paul used concerning slavery. Slaves were to give complete, total obedience to their master. Unfortunately, in Paul's day, many slaves did not get a chance to choose their masters. But we do! Simply put, we can choose righteousness and the way of God, or wickedness and the way of sin. Those are the choices. Whichever choices we make, the master demands our total obedience.

"I want to be free." So the cry goes out. However, the only true freedom we have is to choose to what or to whom we will be slaves. Will it be righteousness or impurity? good or evil? God or ourselves? All of us will serve something or someone. We are free to choose.

## III. Payment (vv. 20-23)

"The wages of sin is death, but the free gift of God is eternal life in Christ Jesus our Lord" (v. 23). In other words, we get a salary for what we do with our lives. We can be slaves to things, but things will not give us love. We can serve pleasure, but its final payment is disillusionment. We can serve our work, but the work will end and we will be forgotten. We can serve ourselves, but we usually are paid back in loneliness and emptiness. Only one way will pay us what we need—that is the way of Christ. Christ brings us life, abundant and eternal. His way will bring us love, mercy, hope, peace, joy, and grace.

It is always our choice. How will we live our lives? What we get out of them in the end depends on what we put into them now. May we choose our pay wisely. (*Hugh Litchfield*)

---

# CHAPTER TWENTY

# LIFE IS UNFAIR?

## PRAYER TO BEGIN WORSHIP

After a week in the world, O God of the sabbath, it is good to return to your sanctuary to retool our bearings. May the words of our pastor and the hymns we sing refresh and quench our thirsty souls. Sometimes we forget that worship is the place where we not only hear the grand stories of our faith, but we can also experience you in holiness and truth. In this hour give us a glimpse of your divine perspective and the hope we need to live out a faithful witness. In Jesus' name we pray. Amen.

## PRAYER OF CONFESSION

O God, who has set his kingdom of heaven here on earth in Jesus Christ, we confess that our vision of your kingdom is shortsighted. We confess, Lord, that we think life should be fair. And we chafe under these expectations when things do not go our way. We look for you, but too easily, we lose our way. And frankly sometimes, we prefer our confusion to the clarity you offer, especially when it comes to our money. Even when we see your desire for our lives, our skeptical spirit and sense of self-security prevents us from embracing your kingdom. We are suspicious of people getting too much of your grace, while at the same time, we feel that we deserve more. We say that we love you, O God, but loving our neighbors as ourselves is difficult for us to achieve, for some of us do not even love ourselves in a healthy way. Yet, in your great wisdom you send Jesus to us to show us that by our own power and might, we can accomplish nothing truly lasting. Rather it is your spirit of grace that opens the possibility of righteousness, of right relationship with you, others, and ourselves. Forgive us. Set us again on the path that leads to you; empower us for the journey. In the name of Jesus, our Savior, we pray. Amen.

## WORDS OF ASSURANCE

Despite all evidence to the contrary, you, O God, Sovereign of the Universe, always promise to be with us. May we live in the confident hope that nothing "in all creation, will be able to separate us from the love of God in Christ Jesus our Lord" (Romans 8:39). This assurance is not from human lips—it is a promise from the very mouth of God. Amen.

## OFFERTORY PRAYER

Benevolent Sovereign, we give our tithes and offering to you in your house because we want to actively participant in something that really matters. As we offer ourselves through these gifts may they remind us that every good and perfect gift comes from you alone. We labor, but only because your labor empowers us. We love, but only because you loved us first. Bless those who receive these gifts and remind us that we are blessed in the giving. In the name of the one who said, "It is more blessed to give than to receive" (Acts 20:35).

## SCRIPTURE: Matthew 20:1-16

# SERMON BRIEF: GOD'S ENDLESS GIVING

"Life is unfair." We hear that blunt statement of reality often in our lives. We have heard it from presidents trying to explain the inequities of political life and from authors trying to help us understand why bad things happen to good people. Parents invoke the statement in attempting to explain the inscrutable complexities of life to their children, and teachers have been known to invoke it when attempting to placate unhappy students.

In this parable from Matthew's Gospel, it appears that Jesus is adding his voice to the many voices over the ages that have intoned: "Life is unfair." The parable of the laborers in the vineyard, as it is best known, is among the more familiar parables of Jesus. A landowner needed workers to pick grapes from his vineyard. Those who did such labor-intensive, seasonal work—then as now—usually were hired from pools of workers who gathered in central locations in hopes of being employed for the day. As more workers were needed, more were hired throughout the day with no specific amount of wages promised to the later workers. The unexpected twist in the story comes when all the workers are given the same wages for vastly different amounts of work. The grumbling begins, and the landowner simply responds by defending his right to be generous.

So often we, especially we who have been pastors, encounter people of faith who feel betrayed by God. They are people who have lived faithfully and worked diligently according to their understanding of God's divine laws. Then life deals them a cruel hand: the untimely death of a loved one, the loss of a job, a devastating illness, or some other tragedy. And, in their understandable anguish, they cry that life is unfair—perhaps even, God is unfair—for they have fulfilled their part of the equation while God has failed to fulfill God's. They become, they believe, the losers in a zero-sum kingdom, a kingdom based on winners and losers, a kingdom based on payment as earned. But Jesus shatters all such notions of God's kingdom in this parable. God's kingdom is not a zero-sum kingdom; it is not a world of merit. It is, instead, a world of grace and mercy where there is more than enough generosity to go around.

Life is unfair. At first glance, that seems to be the message of this parable. But the message is really the complete opposite: life—life in God's kingdom—is more than fair, for God's goodness to us is always far more than we can imagine or deserve. Our economic mindset gets in the way of our understanding of this parable. We are used to systems of merit in which we tally up earnings for work done. But the kingdom of God operates, not on a system of merit, but on a system of abundant grace. The opening lines of a hymn from the Presbyterian Hymnal capture the essence of this parable: "God whose giving knows no ending, From your rich and endless store..." Indeed, God's giving to us is endless. Now God invites us to put our calculators aside, unconcerned about how much we have earned or who is first and who is last, to receive with thanksgiving God's abundant grace and mercy. But not only that: we are also called to remember the word heard in the parable of the unforgiving servant (Matthew 19:23-35), challenging us not to stop with our grateful acceptance of grace and mercy, but to extend it to others. If we are to participate fully in the kingdom proclaimed by Jesus, we cannot help but be generous to others, as God has been generous to us. (*Beverly Zink-Sawyer*)

# CHAPTER TWENTY-ONE

# JOY FULLY SERVING

## INVOCATION

Gracious God, we gather to sing hymns of faith, to pray for our world, and ourselves, and to listen to your Holy Word. Yet we desire far more from you. We desire to open ourselves and experience the full freedom of living a life that really matters. After this past week, with its victories and its disappointments, we all need encouragement and a powerful witness. Free us from a sleepy faith to stand on your promises. In the name of our Redeemer and Sustainer, we pray. Amen.

## PRAYER OF CONFESSION

God of Forgiveness, we approach your throne of grace this morning as a people needing forgiveness. We try to do what is right. And we confess that we believe that if we knew a better way to live our lives, we would do it. Of course, all the while, we also know that Jesus came to show us a more excellent way; and we simply choose not to live his way. We tell white lies, spin the truth, and laugh at unfortunate souls we single out. Still we do not see ourselves as a bad people, so sometimes it is hard to understand that we need your forgiveness. We find ourselves caught between who we think we are and whom we know you

want us to be. Lord, we confess we need help sorting this out. Yet
we fear the pain of seeing ourselves as we truly are. Look into our
hearts, Lord, and make us pure. We claim your promise that those
who are pure in heart will see you. Purify us; cleanse us from all
iniquity; forgive us. Only you can cleanse the glass through which
we see darkly. We yearn to see you face to face. Yet we are too
often afraid of looking each other in the eye. Help us feel the
assurance and acceptance that only you can give. Help us share
your good news with others. Make us your people through the
power of your love. In Jesus' name we pray. Amen.

## WORDS OF ASSURANCE

If you claim the gift and promise of God, then live into Jesus'
words when he told the faithful: "Whoever wants to be first must
be last of all and servant of all" (Mark 9:35). Claim your inheritance as a child of God. Amen.

## PRAYER BEFORE THE READING OF HOLY SCRIPTURE

O God, who inspires the writers of your Holy Scripture,
speak to us through the readings of these sacred texts. Fill us
with the faith we need to live life abundantly and inspire us to
discipleship. Now, may we partake of the wisdom you offer us.
Amen.

## SCRIPTURE: Mark 9:30-37

## SERMON BRIEF: JOY FULLY SERVING

In the comic strip *Calvin and Hobbes*, by Bill Watterson,
Calvin tells Hobbes that people would be less self-centered if
they focused more on others than on themselves. Then Calvin

suggests that everyone simply focus attention on him as an alternative.

Calvin just doesn't get it! Neither did the disciples, according to our Gospel lesson. Jesus is anticipating heading south, toward Jerusalem. He has again talked about how he will suffer. It's important that Jesus and his inner circle be on the same page. The text tells us that, still, the disciples don't understand and are afraid to ask. I remember times when I didn't understand but was afraid to ask—math classes, mostly, in junior and senior high school. I didn't want to come off as more stupid than I already felt!

Maybe the disciples knew so much they were afraid to know any more. It's not unlike the typical response when receiving an alarming diagnosis from a doctor. The news may be so negative that we are afraid to ask any questions; afraid to understand all the details; afraid to know any more. I say that because the text tells us the disciples had been arguing among themselves as to who was the greatest. Could it be that they had understood enough of Jesus' pronouncement to sense his eventual demise so that conversation and conflict had ensued as to who would be best qualified to lead?

We don't know. What Mark does tell us is that when Jesus confronted them they were all too ashamed to reply. They had no defense. So long as they thought Jesus wouldn't know, what did it matter? When in Jesus' presence, the inappropriateness of their behavior was painfully obvious. There is a lesson here, isn't there? When knowing Jesus' presence, our behaviors are likely to be more appropriate, even faithful.

Jesus took their inappropriate behavior seriously because the text says, "He sat down to teach." In his commentary on the Gospel of Mark, biblical theologian William Barclay writes, "When a Rabbi...was teaching as a master teaches his scholars and disciples...he sat to teach" (*The Gospel of Mark* [Philadelphia: The Westminster Press, 1954], 229). When Jesus sat down, it clearly communicated to his disciples that it was time to listen; what follows would be of utmost importance.

And what did he say? If you want to be great in the kingdom it won't come by being first in line, first to be served. Rather you will need to place yourself "last of all and servant of all" (v. 35).

Jesus wasn't against ambition; he refocused it. Instead of ambition to rule, he substituted ambition to serve. Instead of ambition to have things done for us, he substituted ambition to do things for others.

Caregivers who are forever and always doing things for others, even to the point of neglecting self, take note. There is a difference between serving out of a genuine desire to help and helping because of a need to be loved by those you help. Jesus names it later in Mark 12:31 as finding that balance between love of self and love of others.

And, just in case the disciples still hadn't gotten the message, Jesus, knowing that some of them were visual learners, took a child in his lap and said, "Whoever welcomes one such child in my name welcomes me" (v. 37). Jesus didn't give a children's message. The child was the message. The message wasn't that children are the greatest in the kingdom. Rather, all who receive a child will be especially close to Jesus.

A congregation I once served sponsored a breakfast club every weekday morning for "at risk" children, often for as many as two hundred. Studies had shown that a healthy breakfast could raise a child's school performance by as much as 20 percent. Lots of volunteers were required to provide the program, so I took my turn, always reluctantly, out of a sense of duty. I didn't like the wake-up call (we had to be at the church's fellowship hall by 6:30 a.m.), and I didn't like a number of the kids. Too many of them, from my perspective, were rude and ill-mannered.

But one of the volunteers, a retired schoolteacher and a member of the church, was there every day. One morning, I watched as she responded to a child who had just dumped a bowl of oatmeal on a little girl's head. When confronted, the culprit threw a fit. He was out of control: kicking, screaming, and cursing. I watched as this woman hugged the child from behind, sat on the floor with the child between her legs, in what social workers call a "therapeutic hug." She rocked him and sang to him while he continued to throw his fit. Finally, when his rage was spent, he was taken to the time-out room. I said to her, "I don't know how you do it." She replied, "My arms weren't the only arms around that child. Jesus was holding him too. When I added my arms to the circle, I felt especially close to Jesus, and it filled me with joy." She modeled for me that when I serve, however reluctantly, in the name of Jesus, Jesus will be discovered close by. There will then be more than enough joy to serve around. *(Kelly Bender)*

# CHAPTER TWENTY-TWO

# BE EMPOWERED AND GIFTED

## CALL TO WORSHIP: Psalm 104:24-27, 31-33, 35b

O LORD, how manifold are your works!
  In wisdom you have made them all;
  the earth is full of your creatures.
**Yonder is the sea, great and wide,**
  **creeping things innumerable are there,**
  **living things both small and great.**
There go the ships,
  and Leviathan that you formed to sport in it.
**These all look to you**
  **to give them their food in due season;**
May the glory of the LORD endure forever;
  may the LORD rejoice in his works—
**who looks on the earth and it trembles,**
  **who touches the mountains and they smoke.**
I will sing to the LORD as long as I live;
  I will sing praise to my God while I have being.
***All:*** **Bless the LORD, O my soul.**
  **Praise the LORD!**

# PRAYER OF CONFESSION

Eternal God, you who assure us that your grace saves us as we enter that grace by faith, help us rely on your eternal promises. In addition, make us less dependent on the many and various ways our culture lures us from your divine pledge. Jesus asked the disciples, "if the child asks for a fish, [who would give that child] a snake" (from Matthew 7:10)? You, O God, have promised us abundant life, but we, nevertheless, settle for the things that fail to deliver. Again and again and again we seek the promises of those deceivers who do not wish us well. We work and work and work so that we may buy and buy and buy. No matter how hard or long we work, however, the sweat of our brow can never fulfill us as does our completion in your gracious promise of bountiful life in Christ Jesus.

We confess that as we chase the wind, so are our hearts restless for the things that truly gratify. In our lack of divine awareness we continue to pursue a life that we can never attain. Give us the wisdom that satisfies. Give us the excellent judgment to make our way in the world—with joy and thanksgiving to you. Help us, O Divine Master, to gain a heart of vision and insight that will liberate us from the world's shackles. It is upon your mercy alone that we throw ourselves. In the precious name of Jesus we pray. Amen.

# WORDS OF ASSURANCE

"Now faith is the assurance of things hoped for, the conviction of things not seen. Indeed, by faith our ancestors received approval. By faith we understand that the worlds were prepared by the word of God, so that what is seen was made from things that are not visible" (Hebrews 11:1-3). Let us rejoice in God's salvation, which is our assurance. Amen.

# OFFERTORY PRAYER

God of Limitless Grace and Mercy, thank you for the opportunity you give us to offer our bounty and ourselves to the people who need us to share with them as you have first shared with us. Let us remember the words of Paul, who speaks of gifts as "fragrant offering[s], a sacrifice acceptable and pleasing to God" (Philippians 4:18). May you find our gifts and offerings acceptable and pleasing to you, O Lord of the Universe. Amen.

# PASTORAL PRAYER

Almighty God, it is most amazing when we consider the manifold gifts of those sitting with us today in worship. Lord, we want our lives to count. We possess in this household of faith those who can teach, sing, pray, heal, serve, and even preach. Help us use these gifts to be a mighty force for good in this world. Help us do justice, love kindness, and walk humbly with you. We confess that we sometimes tire easily and get distracted by needless worries and worldly cares. Still other times we suffer and cannot shoulder our own share of life's burdens, let alone help shoulder others' burdens. Enable us to harness the power that you have placed at our disposal. Help us yoke ourselves to you, because we know your yoke is easy and your burden is light. Be with us in our times of trial. Free us from our attitude that the world revolves around us. Help us love you more and our possessions less. Help us love you more and ourselves less. Help us love you more so that we can learn what love really means.

Assist in using our gifts wisely. Let us not use them to glorify either our church or ourselves. Rather help us build up the body of Christ so that we may glorify your holy name. Remind us that we are yoked together in this divine adventure because we all drink of the one spirit you offer us as a precious gift. Let there be no gossip, backbiting, or unhealthy discord among us. Let us not speak words that tear down, but only those that lift each other up. Unify our hearts and minds so that we can act as your holy people, dwelling together in peace, harmony, and sanctuary. All this we ask in Christ's holy name. Amen.

## SCRIPTURE: 1 Corinthians 12:3b-13

## SERMON BRIEF: THE GIFTED!

Throughout the book of 1 Corinthians, the apostle Paul addresses a hurting, struggling church. As he moves through his instructions and insights, he comes to a three-chapter segment, chapters 12, 13, and 14, in which he delves into the topic of spiritual gifts. Often we just read the thirteenth chapter. Yet for Paul, that is only the center-piece and not the sum of the whole. With steadily mounting force, his argument is that you and I are the gifted! It is not based on our goodness or our merit but on God's gracious giving.

While our passage begins at verse 3, it must be read in the context of verse 1. "Now concerning spiritual gifts, brothers and sisters, I do not want you to be uninformed." Most of us would rather be called sinners than ignorant, yet it is easy to miss an essential biblical truth about being Christian. Simply put, according to the Bible, if you confess, "Jesus is Lord," you are gifted!

The first point of a sermon might well focus on an understanding of the work of the Holy Spirit in our lives. Through the Holy Spirit, we confess, "Jesus is Lord." We are not gifted based on our goodness, merit, or hard work but through the Spirit's grace.

Verses 4 through 7 forcefully draw our attention to the reason for spiritual gifts. They are for the common good. Verse 7 acts as a summary. "To each is given the manifestation of the Spirit for the common good." In a deeper sense, there is a twin focus here. Each of us is gifted, and the gifts are for the common good. In this one seminal verse, a blow is struck against low self-esteem (which would have us believe that everyone *else* is gifted while we are not), and a blow is struck against any pretensions that spiritual gifts are given for private enjoyment.

I suspect we often fail to perceive ourselves as gifted, because we mistakenly apply this notion of ministry and spiritual gifts only to the clergy. The British army even exempted the clergy from enlistment on their recruiting poster for World War I. We laugh, but all too often the reverse perception is mistakenly held that ministry belongs to the clergy. Biblical reality is far different. Jesus used a number of parables to speak of everyone using their talents or gifts for the work of the Lord. Enshrined in the Protestant Reformation is the principle of the priesthood of all believers. "Now there are varieties of gifts, but the same Spirit; and there are varieties of services, but the same Lord" (vv. 4-5).

In the following verses, each gift is explicitly described as a gift of the Holy Spirit. Thus verse 8 reads: "To one is given through the Spirit the utterance of wisdom, and to another the utterance of knowledge according to the same Spirit." Furthermore, the list of gifts in verses 8 through 10 is only the beginning. There are a number of other biblical lists of spiritual gifts. Some scholars are convinced that Paul deliberately leaves the list open-ended by way of demonstrating that there are many gifts and that all of God's people are gifted.

One afternoon while viewing Boston Harbor from an over-look, I was fortunate to watch a race of large sailing ships. As they rounded a buoy marking the course, the wind caught the vessels directly from behind. With precision, accuracy, and speed, the crews unfurled a sail on the bow, which billowed outward catching the wind. Such was the power of the sail catching the wind that the ships almost leaped forward in the water.

This is a reflection of the image Paul unfolds for us in this passage. All are gifted! That means all of us are gifted for the work of ministry! This is the presence, the manifestation or making known, of the Holy Spirit's presence in our lives both individually and as a community of faith.

One of the ancient symbols for the Christian church was a ship with its sails unfurled. Such is the image for any church when we employ our spiritual gifts properly. We surge forward, catching the full wind of the Holy Spirit. It can only happen with the helmsman and the crew working in graceful precision as they accomplish the mission entrusted. We know the helmsman; it is Jesus our Lord. Jesus' wind, the wind of the Holy Spirit, gusts across our community calling us to unfurl our sails.

Using verse 7 as the key verse, a sermon could be built on three points: (1) Spiritual gifts are a work of the Holy Spirit; (2) All are gifted; (3) Our gifts are to be used for the common good. (*Mike Lowry*)

# CHAPTER TWENTY-THREE

# JESUS WAS NO FOOL

## INVOCATION

Gracious God, we ask you this day to warm our hearts and encourage our spirits as we worship and magnify your holy name. In our hour of worship show us symbols and signs of your holy presence among us. Grant us the insight to relate the words of sacred Scripture to the living of our day-to-day lives. Make us attentive to the divine message that can make our mundane world such a joy. In the name of Christ, we pray. Amen.

## PRAYER OF CONFESSION

God of Wisdom, we confess that far too often we have behaved like those who questioned Jesus: "Is it lawful to pay taxes to the emperor, or not?" We struggle with knowing to whom we owe allegiance. Do we owe our ultimate allegiance to family or community? to nation or church? to our work or our family? By these questions, Lord, we put off declaring where our ultimate allegiance really lies. Help us understand that by setting up counterfeit choices in life we often become like those who tell Paul after he preached the gospel in Athens: "We will hear you again about this" (Acts 17:32). Our desire to revisit the gospel—Sunday after Sunday—is simply our polite way of saying we cannot make up our minds. How long, O Lord, can we "go limping with two different opinions" (1 Kings 18:21)?

Help us, we beg you, O Sovereign One. Give us singleness of heart. Help us obey Christ as Christ was obedient to death. Offer to us that word of assurance that our lives, lived in your divine purposes, will not be lived in vain. Offer us words of promise in ways that we can apprehend and obey in cheerfulness and thanksgiving. You, as our heavenly parent, have offered us untold riches in the gospel of Jesus Christ. Give us the will and heart to submit ourselves to the yoke that Christ offers us in freedom from sin even as he offers us the cost of discipleship as stewards of your grace. In all things, may we be a thankful people who offer your divine blessing to our world in need. Amen.

# WORDS OF ASSURANCE

"As a father has compassion for his children, so the Lord has compassion for those who fear him. For he knows how we were made; God remembers that we are dust" (Psalm 103:13-14). Remember that our Lord is our strength and shield, our rock and our redeemer. Amen.

# PRAYER OF THANKSGIVING

O God of the gracious gift of life, we assemble today out of gratitude for the many and various ways that your grace interconnects with our lives. Too often we fail to express our gratitude to you at all; yet we recognize that worship allows us to convey the heartfelt thanksgiving we feel. We ask that our voices join other believers around the world, as well as the saints throughout the ages as our prayers ascend beyond the crowns of the clouds and reach unto the holy places where you, O Most High, make your home. Yet, as you transcend our human realm, we recognize that you mercifully live immanently within us and intimately among us. Make us a living portrait of your loving mercy that you yearn to communicate to our hurting world. Let us be the disciples you have equipped us to become. We pray this and every prayer in the merciful name of Jesus, our Lord and Advocate. Amen.

## SCRIPTURE: Matthew 22:15-22

## SERMON BRIEF: OF WISDOM AND MONEY

Jesus was no fool: he knew a trap when he saw one and responded accordingly. In this Gospel lesson, Jesus escapes entrapping questions intended to destroy by turning them into answers intended to puzzle. "Give therefore to the emperor the things that are the emperor's," Jesus says (v. 21). Rather than debating whether Caesar's face on the coin is idolatrous or paying taxes is unjust, Jesus reminds the listeners that money is symbolic and temporary. This lesson is lost on far too many people. Money is gained and accumulated for any number of reasons but almost always with the idea that it will last as long as it is tended carefully. Anyone who has watched stock portfolios change in this decade certainly has learned that such is not always the case! Still, people hoard money and manage it as if it were a permanent fixture on this earth. Jesus reminds us that this simply is not true.

Likewise, Jesus reminds us that God is invested in the permanent fixtures of our lives. It may be less clear what those permanent fixtures are, but we could venture some educated guesses: our lives, our faith, and our souls. All of these are the very stuff of which God made us, and thus "things that are God's." Yet, even the impermanent things of this life belong to God as they pass through our lives: time, talents, skills, passions, ideas, and material gifts (including money).

Still, Jesus relegates those impermanent things to their proper place, as being a part of this earthly world, important symbols, but not the stuff of which God made us. Woven carefully, these contrasting themes (giving the permanent fixtures of our lives alongside the impermanent things of this life to God) can be woven into a challenging stewardship sermon.

However, Jesus' wisdom and care, in not regarding people with partiality as he converses with his adversaries, might also bring a powerful message to light. Here, Jesus speaks as respectfully of the Roman emperor as he does of God, not a common courtesy that most of his religious colleagues would have given to Caesar. Likewise, even as Jesus criticizes the Pharisees and Herodians, Jesus criticizes his own disciples. To all of them, he says "Why are you putting me to the test, you hypocrites?" (v. 18). And to all of them, Jesus offers a wise but puzzling answer about coins and emperors and God—a warning to the "would-be wise." However, Jesus stands alone after this difficult conversation. When everyone hears Jesus' amazing words, they leave him and go away. Such is the journey of many wise followers of God, and such may be our path when we, too, seek the wisdom of God and share it with others. But knowing that this wisdom comes from and belongs to God, we have no choice but to share it with others, for how else can we give that which belongs to God back to God but to share it with God's people—even if it means standing alone when all is said and done. *(Mary J. Scifres)*

# BENEDICTION

May you leave this place with the blessed assurance that you are never alone. May you go into the world knowing that your life with God counts.

# Scripture Index